THE SP

# TONY DE
# MELLO

# THE SPIRIT OF
# TONY DE MELLO

## A HANDBOOK OF MEDITATION EXERCISES

### JOHN CALLANAN, SJ

# MERCIER PRESS

**Mercier Press**
5 French Church Street, Cork
24 Lower Abbey Street, Dublin 1

© John Callanan 1993

ISBN 1 85635 044 4

*A CIP is available for this book from the British Library.*

*To my parents, and all those who
encourage others to soar like an eagle,
rather than remain earth-bound like the
chicken-bird.*

*Printed in Ireland by Colour Books Ltd.*

# Contents

# Acknowledgements

Many people helped me to get started on this book. I thank first my parents, family and Jesuit brothers who gave me the sort of start which made it possible to appreciate the spirit that Tony de Mello imparted. I thank also Fr Eddie O'Donnell, SJ, who was a constant source of encouragement and who undertook the frightening task of correcting my scripts; Fr Donal Neary, SJ, and two other friends, Carmel and Vera, for being constant friends and an inspiration to write; my brother Bill, also a Jesuit, who drew the illustrations; and my team-mates in Tabor Retreat House who put up with me and tested out some of the prayer exercises during various retreats. I thank them also for their coaxing and cajoling, without which I would never have started.

# Introduction

Many people can remember where they were when John F. Kennedy was shot. I remember equally well the place and time I heard that Fr Tony de Mello, SJ, had died. I was in Bolivia, eagerly awaiting a return to Ireland so that I could attend Fr Tony's latest Irish retreat workshop when word reached me of his unexpected demise. To say I was stunned is an under-statement. My first thought was 'What a shame'. He had inspired so many people – including me. At that moment I felt it might be worthwhile to jot down what I could recall of his retreats and workshops.

This book is the fruit of those memories. It is also an attempt to capture some of the essence and spirit of the man himself. Tony de Mello was a great teacher. He taught through lectures, retreats, videos and books, using a blend of spirituality, stories and jokes that stayed with the listener. His stories and jokes always had a point to them. When the story got across we were suddenly exposed in our ambition, our pettiness, our stupidity, our superficiality or our self-complacency. Because of the fun element within the jokes or stories we were able to laugh, even at ourselves. We laughed and we learned. Some said Tony was not only a great teacher but also a dangerous one. He constantly challenged himself, the world within which he lived and consequently those he came into contact with. For some this element of challenge is both unsettling and confusing. Tony taught that our security does not lie in thoughts or ideas no matter how profound. Neither does it lie in traditions – no matter how hallowed. Security, if there be any, can only reside in an attitude of mind and a readiness to reflect deeply, thus subjecting any and every belief to rigorous questioning. So Tony urged us to question, question, question. And questions often make us uncomfortable. They do, however, force us to reflect and thus ensure our growth.

The book is aimed at those who know little or nothing of Tony de Mello or his work. It is also for those who have read some of his books but may like or need an incentive to go back and read them again. Tony himself recommended that both his exercises and many of his books be read in small doses. I can do no better than to quote his own advice in this regard. He suggested that his stories could be read in three ways:

> 1. *Read the story once. Then move on. This manner of reading will give you entertainment.*
> 2. *Read a story twice. Reflect on it. Apply it to your life.*
> 3 *Read a story again, after you have reflected on it. Create a silence within you and let the story reveal to you its inner depth and meaning: something beyond words and reflections. This will give you a feel for the mystical. Or carry the story around all day and allow its fragrance, its melody to haunt you. Let it speak to your heart, not to your brain. This too could make something of a mystic out of you. It is with this mystical end in view that most of these stories were originally told.*

So it is with this book. I recommend you start with Chapter 1 even though it may be the most tedious or the most difficult. Practice stilling yourself, becoming aware, and attempt the listening and breathing exercises because I will be recommending that you try these at the beginning of most of the Fantasy exercises or Gospel meditations which I have included in this book. The exercises themselves are, by and large, not Tony de Mello's own but are based mainly on the style he suggested. The exercises are ones which I and others have put together and found useful over eight years or so of retreats and workshops and are based on the prayer-style which Tony himself developed during his retreats.

Where possible, I have tried to credit those upon whose original ideas the meditation or fantasy exercise is based, but, by their very nature, many of these exercises tend to change or are adapted over time. Thus, I ask forgiveness from those whose ideas or presentations I have borrowed, as I have now forgotten where many of the ideas came from originally.

Many who knew Tony found him a fund of encouragement and insight in their own lives. Biographical details about him are rare but he himself said that some of his insights were possibly developed from his earliest childhood experiences in India. There he was exposed to Hindu and Buddhist cultures as well as to Christianity. He was fortunate enough as a young Jesuit to be sent to Spain in order that he might study philosophy. There he was greatly influenced by some of the Christian mystics including Teresa of Avila and

John of the Cross. Subsequently, he was sent by his Jesuit superiors to study psychology in the United States. In his workshops and retreats the insightful blending of Eastern and Western spirituality combined with a knowledge and awareness of the psychological dimension of human nature provided a heady cocktail.

However, his early years as a priest could not have foretold where his thinking was to lead. During that period of his life he found himself appointed novice-master in India and, in his own words, was, during that time, both conventional and strict. I recall one story he told about his novice-master days. Shortly after he came on the job he found he was shocked by many of the novices' ideas of how they might live out their vow of poverty. To rectify this he called the novices together and told them that the variety and number of clothes they seemed to possess was more than he could countenance. He suggested that after prayers that night each novice should go to his room and bring downstairs all articles of clothing which they felt they might do without. These would be collected the next day and given to a local charity. That night a wonderful collection of garments appeared in the common-room. One brother-novice who was present later told Tony that he slipped down to the common-room after the others had gone to bed and took away for himself anything decent he could find. He was, he said, desperately short of some decent apparel. When Tony recounted the story later, he ended his account by saying, 'Well, at least one of us had some sense'.

Fr Tony de Mello had the gift of bringing life

wherever he went. This was never more evident to me than on his first visit to Ireland in 1977. He had made a huge impact on the thirty-second General Congregation of the Jesuits in Rome in 1975, so the Irish Provincial invited him to address us at the Retreat House in Rahan, County Offaly. The participants were there to take part in one of his week-long retreats. He burst on the scene with amazing freshness. The spirit he managed to produce on that first evening was astounding. Straightaway his listeners were challenged to their very limits and many spent the entire evening spellbound. At two subsequent retreats and prayer-workshops that I attended in Ireland and California the effect was identical. What he preached shocked many to the core, but left a thirst for life which remains to this day. Whilst some disagreed with what he had to say, I think very few were unmoved.

I know I need to go back to his books, audio and video cassettes at regular intervals to refresh myself with a sense of his spirit and spirituality. Many people have told me on retreats and workshops that they find such refresher courses equally useful. For those of you who know little or nothing about Tony de Mello, I hope this book will encourage you to read and savour his original texts. The names of these are included in the bibliography. For those of you who know a good deal about Tony and his teachings already, I hope that by recapturing some of Tony's spirit in this book you may be encouraged to return to the sources for refreshment and renewal. My hope is that interest and enthusiasm for Tony de Mello's work and insights may be furthered in this way.

To assist those who might like to try out Tony's prayer style for themselves and for those who use his material and spiritual insights by leading prayer-group sessions, I have started the book with an opening chapter on the basics of prayer. I moved on from there to try and give a flavour of the ideas and themes which gave so much zest and life to Tony de Mello's presentations.

As a further assistance to those same readers, I have included at the end of each chapter a selection of prayer exercises, meditations and fantasy inputs which may help prayer guides become familiar with Fr Tony's style of prayer.

Tony de Mello died suddenly in New York on 2 June 1987 while conducting a prayer workshop in Fordham University. He had spent himself to the full, but his spirit lives on. I see this book as a tribute to his zest for life.

*Fr John Callanan, SJ*

# 1

# Learning the Basics

Fr Tony de Mello used to tell us that in his younger days he had spent a certain amount of time on retreats based on the Buddhist style of prayer. In these retreats, the participants concentrated a great deal of their time on breathing and breath control. One of Tony's favourite sayings was, 'Your breath is your greatest friend', and at the beginning of each retreat or workshop which I attended under his guidance he would spend a good deal of time explaining the whole process of breath control, quietening, becoming aware, and creating the conditions whereby one might meet God. In this first chapter I hope to be equally practical and I lay out some basic steps which an individual or group might follow if they wish to pray in the way Tony suggested. At the end of each chapter I offer a *Gospel Meditation* or *Fantasy Exercise* and I suggest you prepare yourself for the period of prayer through an exercise such as the one described below.

## Preparatory Exercise

Settle yourself comfortably in your favourite prayer place and, with your eyes closed, begin to still your mind. Try to do this by withdrawing from the world

around you and attempt to let go of all distractions. At first, this will not be easy. You will be
bombarded with all sorts of idle thoughts and mind
wanderings, such as,
'What do I need to buy
for this evening's tea?' or
'Have I turned off the
gas?' but after some time
you will be able to leave
these distractions aside.
Gradually, turn your at-
tention to your breath-
ing. Gently breathe in
through your nostrils,
drawing the breath right
down to the pit of your
stomach. Many people
are helped here by imag-
ining that as they draw
the breath right into
their body, they are
drawing either the Spirit
of God, or possibly a
gentle mist or colour
right inside themselves.

As you attempt this exercise, imagine that you
are breathing the colour yellow inside yourself as
you breathe in. As the breath enters, picture in
your mind's eye the image of yellow smoke beginning to swirl through your nostrils, hitting the
back of your throat, coming down your neck and
around your shoulders, down your arms and into
your chest before circling around your backbone
and then reaching the very pit of your stomach,

where you can feel it if you put your hand gently over your belly-button.

Now exhale gently, letting go of all the stale air or imagining that the yellow colour or mist is departing from your body, starting from the pit of your stomach and gently vacating your stomach area before moving back up to your chest, then up to your arms and shoulders, up through the neck region and out through your lips.

It sometimes helps this breathing exercise if you count to yourself as you do it saying: 'Now I breathe in and now I breathe out, two, three, four', or again, 'Breathing Christ in, breathing worry out', or again, 'Breathing goodness in', and hold gently for four or five seconds, 'Breathing trouble out', letting go of all the stale air inside your body, before quietly taking in your next breath. As you undertake the exercise, become aware of the sense of calm that starts to settle upon you.

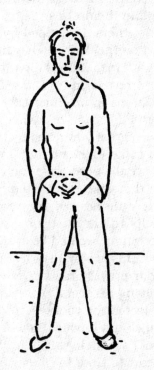

# Selecting a Place for Prayer

As the object of meditation is to find the silence within, thereby finding God, or letting Him find you, select a place where you are not likely to be disturbed. Some people find that if they set aside a corner of their room and perhaps place one of their favourite pictures or icons along with a candle there, it will help them to build an inner stillness within themselves.

Others are helped by a quiet room with a carpet on the floor for they find they can meditate best in a horizontal position. I attended Tony de Mello's first retreat in Ireland with three Jesuits who lived with me in an Inner City Dublin flat. When we returned to our residence we realised that we had been greatly touched by the encounter. We decided to come together each morning to see if we could mutually encourage each other by praying together in the same room. That mutual support, added to the quietness of the room we used, was a great help to us in trying to follow the meditation technique we had been shown by Tony.

This is why I suggest that, in the early stages of your prayer practice, you may be greatly helped by having a special place for prayer which you have selected for yourself. This place should be warm, quiet and private. Such a spot often sets up associations which will help you turn your mind and heart to God. In time, you will feel that the vibrations are good in that place and your prayer base will be linked in your mind with a sense of inner peace.

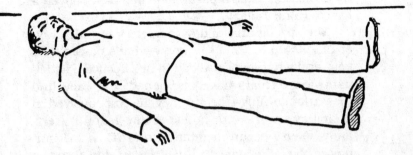

So establish the place and include within it a kneeler, rug, icon, cross and Bible along with incense and a small lamp or candle if these additions help you. It depends on how much you are affected by your surroundings, for many of us are much influenced by atmosphere whilst others are not really bothered by their surroundings. Try out the above suggestions for yourself so as to discover what works for you. One last tip. In order to ensure peace, take the phone off the hook before starting.

## Selecting a Time for Prayer

Whatever type of journey you are engaged upon, it helps to keep some kind of timetable if you hope to travel successfully. Something similar applies in prayer. If you can set aside a regular time each day for your efforts, the discipline involved in sticking to that will aid you. Try to allocate a specific length of time – say, half an hour – and the habit will ensure that you yourself know that this is your prayer time and before long others will know too that you prefer not to be disturbed then. The very routine of setting aside a particular time has a psychological value in itself.

The special time of day you select as your prayer time is up to you. You know what's possible for you, and what is most likely to be effective. Participants on retreats have mentioned that they find the early morning – before they become involved in their day's work – to be especially helpful. Certainly when I began meditation myself, as a Jesuit novice, we all engaged in meditation first thing in the morning on the general theory that one's mind is freshest then. Besides, the dangers of neglecting it if left until later in the day are very real. Essentially, however, the best time for prayer is the time that suits you best, so stay with what works and is most practical for you. As you start out on the journey you may feel that not much is happening for you, but look upon the time spent as a sort of 'recharging the batteries' time and before long, profit will ensue.

Over the past few years, a number of Jesuits and their friends have been asked how they pray and what tips they have to offer on the subject. I include some of their comments here in the hope that, as they helped me, they may also help you. One of these people mentioned that praying has gone through four phases for him. 'First, I talked at God. Then I talked to God. Then I listened to God. Now I listen for God'. When asked why they prayed, those questioned suggested the following reasons: 'Firstly, because God never ceases to stir up in me urgent longings to be more intimate with Him and more interior to myself than I usually am. Secondly, talking to others about their prayer moves me deeply and stirs me to pray myself if for no other reason than to maintain my own credibility. Finally, I truly believe from experience that prayer constitutes my major avenue towards entering my deepest self – the part of me where God meets my inner spirit. In prayer I place myself in the presence of God and ask myself the question, what is it I want from God this day? This question necessarily calls me to preview my day, trying to foresee the people with whom I will be dealing, the places I will go, the activities in which I will be involved. As my mind rapidly passes over all of this matter, I may find myself asking God's help in a myriad of details which fill the screen of my life this day. The question drives me deep into the stillness of my heart. What is it that I ask of the Lord this day? And as I ask the question I find myself becoming quiet. Probably my best prayer comes after some experience which has strongly affected me. I need to reflect before God on that experience, get in touch with my feelings about it, understand more deeply its meaning for my future. Even when I go through periods of non-prayer, I know that God is tremendously courteous, never forcing Himself on me. He waits like a patient friend'.

May he also wait for you.

## Meditation
*The Prodigal Son*

This meditation will be helped if you settle yourself comfortably, close your eyes, and prepare yourself by means of one of the preparatory exercises.

**Step 1:**

Read the Gospel story of the Prodigal Son (Luke 15: 2–32).

Situate the Gospel story for yourself, picturing the Prodigal Son with his father. You might want to become that son or daughter yourself. The Prodigal does not accept himself for some reason. Perhaps he has ingrained within himself feelings of poor self-worth, or feels these messages had been dumped upon him by others. For some months now, he has been uneasy, feels left out, unsure of what to do with himself, doubtful about his future prospects and quite uncertain about which direction his future life should take. He knows that the longer he feels excluded from his family the more painful life becomes. Perhaps he will never again regain feelings of 'all rightness' about himself. To whom should he turn? At last he decides to take desperate action.

*First Reflective Pause:*

Lord, I pause here and think of the times I have excluded myself from situations or people. Yet you constantly held out a hand to me, drawing me back. Let me be grateful for that. (Stay with that image for as long as it feels profitable and then move on.)

**Step 2:**

Meanwhile, outside on the farm, the Prodigal's father is working away. He realises what his son is going through and his only desire is that he can somehow reach his son. The old man is sensitive.

He wishes his son to be free, and fears crushing his spirit, knowing that the boy must come to his own decisions and choose his own inner life patterns. Then, one morning, the Prodigal son wakes up and life has suddenly become too painful, so he goes to his father, and taking his courage in his hands, begins to stammer out his demands. 'Father, give me my share of the inheritance now.'

Note the beautiful response of the father. He takes stock of his property and hands over half his possessions ... and so the younger son goes ... enjoying ... spending ... trying to fill the void.

*Second Reflective Pause:*

Lord, forgive me for the times I grabbed all around me and tried to fill a void with worldly goods. Let me muse over the times this happened with my life over the past year. (When I feel I have got what benefit I can from this I continue.)

**Step 3:**
So the Prodigal son leaves home, on his wild search for meaning, but of that he finds nothing. Only isolation, and pain, and an inner emptiness.

*Third Reflective Pause:*

Lord, forgive me for the times I held on to pains and hurts and refused either to forgive myself or to accept the forgiveness you held out to me ... but as the younger son begins to look inside himself he realises that there may be a way out of his pain ... and that instead of looking outside himself for the relief and meaning which he requires in his life he begins to gaze inwards instead ... he remembers the times when he has felt forgiven ... when his father used to hold him in his arms ... all the things the father used to say to him ... and these very remembrances help him realise that there may yet be a way back for him ... if he can only return to that source of goodness and love in his life ... he begins to think that maybe he's better than he thought he was ... and thus, with trepidation, he begins to turn his face towards home ...

*Fourth Reflective Pause:*

Lord, help me to regain my nerve if I have lost it ... help me to realise and to believe that if I turn back to the source of life I may again find meaning and hope.

Now the younger son didn't realise it, but as he turned back his action was the very thing the father longed and prayed for ... each day the father would go out to the highest hill near the farm and search in the distance looking for his son ... and there was only one thought in the father's heart ... 'I want my son back'... and then one day, suddenly, the father sees the faintest shape in the distance ... and you can imagine the hope and the love that wells up in his heart ... and running as fast as his old legs can carry him, he reaches the place where his son is along the road ... and he wraps his arms around the young son, and the prodigal, falling to his knees, and still not sure of the father's forgiveness, says, 'Father, I have no rights left. I have come begging for forgiveness' ...

but as soon as the prodigal looks up into the father's eyes he sees there only one expression ... love ... the delight at having the boy back again ... and it's difficult for the prodigal to allow himself to be forgiven ... but when he feels the negative memories of his past coming to the surface ... any memories of what he may have done wrong before ... he just remembers that sight of his father rushing down from the hill towards him ... and holding him ... and he goes over that scene so often in his mind that the very memory of it begins to heal him ...

*Fifth Reflective Pause:*

And I also, Lord, begin to realise how you might have worked upon me in my past and forgiven me for any transgressions that I may have done ... and even though I may be tempted to hold on to some of the old negative images I pray now that the memory of you holding out your hand of forgiveness to me will begin to heal me and allow me to know in my heart that I am forgiven.

And so, resting in the knowledge that the Father loves and cares for me, I bring the meditation to a close.

## Fantasy Exercise

*The Joyful, Sorrowful, and Glorious Mysteries of my Life.*

We all carry within us an album of snapshots of the past. They are memories of events that formed us. In your imagination, open this album now and recall some of these events. It will take time but gradually you will discover memories buried away. So unearth them and relive them in the presence of the Lord.

### Step 1:

Having prepared yourself for prayer, return in memory to a scene in which you felt deeply loved, esteemed and cared for. Recall the circumstances, the people, the feelings and become aware of the presence of God in this scene. Thank Him for the occasion, and ask a blessing on those who shared the moment with you. If you are completing this exercise with a group, you might ask them to write in their 'magic' moments on the petals of the 'glorious' flower which accompanies this exercise.

### Step 2:

Recall some scene where you felt pain or bitterness and relive that scene also. Try to see the presence of the Lord in that event also. Imagine He is taking part in it with you. Speak to Him. Ask why the event is happening and what meaning it might have for you. Try to forgive the people who caused you pain and pray for them. Write down the painful memories in the petals of the 'sorrowful' flower.

### Step 3:

Now conjure up in your imagination a scene which was joyful for you. What good news have you heard, or what desire has been fulfilled? Linger on that scene and thank and praise God for it. Relive the scene and allow it to make you more conscious of the part the Lord has played in those events.

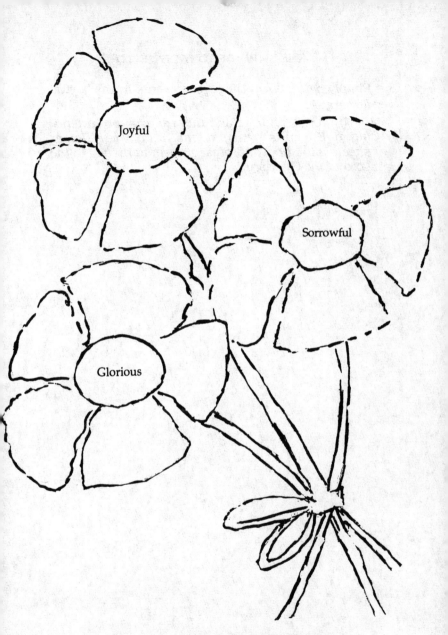

*My life ... its joyful, sorrowful mysteries*
– reflect and mark in on each petal.

Finally, write down the joyous events in the 'joyful' flower.

*If groups undertaking this exercise are attending a Eucharist, they might bring their flower sheets with them and present them in thanks to the Lord at the Offertory.*

# 2

# Heart of Silence

When coming to Christ, we try to create an atmosphere of prayer. But what is prayer? Some people think it's a raising up of the mind and heart to God, or just talking to God, or perhaps some form of union with God. However you define it, prayer would appear to have three elements: God, yourself, and the relationship between God and yourself.

First, let us consider God, and what we know of Him. Who or what is He? Thomas Aquinas used to say that the only thing we can say with certainty is that we do not know God. Tony de Mello said something similar on his first retreat workshop with us. When asked who God is, he'd say: 'I don't know. Nobody knows'. It seems clear to me that we have built up pictures or images of who or what God might be and because these pictures or images may not be at all helpful to us in our dealings with God, a certain amount of 'unlearning' may now be vital for us. It is necessary to go beyond words or images and to seek God deep within the silence which resides within us. During the early part of our retreat, Tony concentrated a lot on silence. He would try to bring his listeners to an awareness of their own innermost being. To explain this point, Tony would tell a story.

One day, the local governor was passing close to where a wise and holy Zen Master lived and, as he passed, he began to speak to the Master asking him to explain the meaning of religion in one sentence. 'I can do better, I can give it to you in one word,' said the Master. 'It can be summed up in the word Silence.'

'But how can I get silence?' asked the Governor.

'Meditation,' came the reply. 'And what is meditation?' asked the Governor.

'Silence,' said the Zen Master.

Tony, in his workshops, would seldom try to describe God. In fact, he often mentioned that attempting such a description was often more unhelpful than helpful to his listeners. He just encouraged us to 'be' before the Lord and by that he meant placing ourselves silently in God's presence and just being with Him. Thus, for Tony, the foundation for prayer must, in some way, be the incomprehensibility of God.

It may be helpful at this point to think about someone born blind. Such a person might well ask a sighted friend to explain a concept such as colour or smell to them. But how can one explain such a concept? It is of little use to try and ask a sightless person to imagine how crystal blue a certain patch of sea looks, or how beautifully the colours in a landscape merge.

So it is with human beings when they try to describe in words the God they are trying to communicate with. The task they have set themselves is impossible, and perhaps even unhelpful. God is beyond our limited human minds.

As Tony put it to us during that first Irish retreat, 'God cannot be known, but he can be recognised'. Just think of the disciples on the road to Emmanus. Though they didn't know Jesus, they recognised something vital as it entered their lives. Indeed Tony challenged us on this point. 'The Messiah came,' he said, 'but his own failed to recognise him.' Perhaps 'religious' people may fail to spot Jesus when He comes into their lives. If we are inoculated with large doses of religion we may fail to notice the genuine article when it appears. We search for our God in scripture, in books, in retreats and the like while all the time our God is right around us. To illustrate this point, Tony used to quote a line from the poet Kabil, 'I laughed when they told me that the fish in the water was thirsty'. Perhaps we too have been searching for God in multitudes of places but have lost him in our hearts?

At this point in his Irish retreats Tony de Mello introduced a novel concept. He began by explaining that St Paul prepared himself to meet his God – or was so prepared – by persecuting the very followers of the one he would ultimately follow. In some strange fashion, therefore, it may be that the best preparation for meeting or finding God is this: to recognise more and more that we are sinners – 'Where sin increased, God's grace increased much more' (Romans 5:20). Put another way, it may well be that sinful people – or at least the ones who know they are sinful – may have a greater hunger and need for their Lord than those who think they are worthy followers of Christ.

How can we assist ourselves to become conscious of God in our lives? Well, being constantly attentive might help us. To get some notion of the degree of attention which we're talking about here, you might think of a time when you travelled abroad and had to spend some time alone. For example, you might have travelled alone by train during the night over difficult and dangerous terrain. Remember the great effort when you tried to stay awake to keep an eye over your possessions – most particularly your passport and money. Not a moment went by but your senses were on alert. You knew you could not afford to lose any of your vital documents and thus, despite the tiredness, you somehow managed to keep your eyes open. If you have been in this situation, you know that you were constantly looking around you, keeping your wits about you and ever on the look-out for shady-looking characters. Similarly, in our prayer lives, we strive for that same degree of attention, constantly on the look-out for signs of the Spirit in our day-to-day existence.

## Exercise for Sharpening Awareness

Having prepared yourself for prayer, concentrate on the slightest sensations and sounds around you. Feel the air passing through your nostrils. Focus on one small area of your body. When Tony de Mello did this exercise with us during workshops, he asked us to concentrate on a single part of our bodies. He would suggest focusing on a very small area, about the size of a postage stamp, in the very middle of our foreheads. Try to be aware of every sensation there. Whilst breathing, concentrate on inhalation or exhalation alone particularly if you are bothered by distractions.

*Note: At the end of this exercise, some participants would explain that they found this whole process extremely difficult. I know that I myself could experience little or no conscious sensations in this small forehead space for ages and ages. Some people would admit that they felt during the exercise that they had been forcing themselves, but Tony would tell them not to worry. Just continue being faithful to the exercise, he would say, and in time you will have your reward. That same advice I pass on to you and I think that, in time, you will find his encouragement is both valid and true. Stay with the exercise for a time and take it gently. Do not force yourself. Violence is no help for it is better to get around an obstacle than to crash through it. Take the session at your own pace and if you are finding it difficult try to ascertain what is causing the blockage within you. Ask yourself 'what is making me tense?' By doing this, insight may come. When you sense what is happening, the problem may disappear without you having to do anything about it.*

## Excercise of Reconciliation

This exercise is one we used for Youth and Community Groups in the Tabor Youth Retreat House, the outline of which we had been given by groups in County Limerick.

*Preparation*
First gather the group together in a darkened room with a large Taize Cross in the centre of the floor and with Taize music playing in the background. Incense may also be used and if the participants are seated on the floor they will normally appreciate it.
*Opening Music/Hymn. (Perhaps 'Stay Here', a cas-*

*sette music tape from the youth centre of Taize in France, would be appropriate.)*

**Celebrant:** (We pray now for true conversion, first in silence.) Almighty and merciful God, you bring us together in the name of your Son and in the power of your Spirit. Open our eyes to see the evil we have done. Touch our hearts and convert us to you so that we might live free from sin and free for you. We ask this in Jesus' name.

**All:** Amen.

## Celebration of the Word of God

**N:** (First speaker) There was once a man who had two sons. The younger said to his father:

**PS:** Father, give me my share of the property now.

**N:** So the man divided the property between his two sons.

**PS:** After a few days the younger son sold his part of the property and left home with the money. He went to a country far away, where he wasted his money in reckless living.

*Note. After each section of scripture text, a number of petitions are spoken aloud, based on the text which has just been heard. After the petitions, the Taize tape which has been lowered for the script-ure text and the petitions can resume for about half a minute to allow both the text and petitions to sink in before the celebrant continues with the next sec-tion of scripture text.*

## Petitions

**Speaker 1:** Father, we pray for those who are try-ing to find life apart from you.

**All:** Lord have mercy.

**Speaker 1/2:** Father, we pray for those who have taken the gifts you have given them for granted, and who have used them selfishly and carelessly.

**All:** Christ have mercy.

**Speaker 1/2/3:** Father, we pray for ourselves now, too. A part of us is like the prodigal son. We bring that part of us to you now for healing. *(Brief pause for personal prayers for healing and forgiveness.)*

**N:** The younger son spent everything he had. Then a severe famine spread over that country, and he was left without a thing. So he went to work for one of the citizens of that country, who sent him out to his farm to take care of the pigs. He wished he could fill himself with the bean pods that the pigs themselves ate, but no one gave him anything to eat.

## Petitions

**Speaker 1:** Father, we pray for those who feel forsaken, alone, or troubled. Lord, have mercy.

**All:** Lord, have mercy.

**Speaker 1/2:** Father, we pray for those whose human dignity is violated by being treated in inhuman ways.

**All:** Christ have mercy.

**Speaker 1/2/3:** Father, we now want to pray for ourselves. We know how it feels to be alone and troubled. We bring you our pain which now needs to be healed. *(Brief pause for personal prayers of healing and forgiveness.)*

**N:** At last the younger son came to his senses and began to say to himself:

**PS:** All my father's hired workers have more than

they can eat, and here I am about to starve. I will get up and go to my father and say to him, Father, I have sinned against heaven and before you. I am no longer fit to be called your son; treat me as one of your hired workers.

## Petitions

**Speaker 1:** Father, we pray for those in whom your light is dawning, who are coming to recognise the gifts that you have given them. Lord, have mercy.

**Speaker 1/2:** Father, we pray for those who long to know their sin and have the strength to change their lives. Christ have mercy.

**Speaker 1/2/3:** Father, part of us is still broken and yet repentant. We pray for ourselves and we bring to you all that is broken within us asking for your healing and forgiveness. *(Brief pause for personal prayer.)*

**N:** So the younger son got up and started back to his father. He was still a long way from home when his father saw him; the father's heart was filled with pity, and he ran, and threw his arms around his son, and kissed him.

Then the younger son said, 'Father, I have sinned against God and against you. I am no longer fit to be called your son.'

But the father called his servants. 'Hurry,' he said, 'bring the best robe and put it on him. Put a ring on his finger and shoes on his feet. Then go and get the prize calf and kill it: and let us celebrate with a feast. For this son of mine was dead, but now he is alive. He was lost, but now is found.'

**Speaker 1:** Father, we pray for those who cannot

be a father like this and who are over-demanding and critical.

**All:** Lord, have mercy.

**Speaker 1/2:** Father, we pray for all those who feel that they have had to earn your forgiveness, and so never really feel forgiven.

**All:** Christ, have mercy.

**Speaker 1/2/3:** Father, a part of us longs for forgiveness, while a part of us already experiences forgiveness. We pray now for our divided selves that you would heal us and make us whole in the image of your Son. *(Brief pause for personal prayers of healing and forgiveness.)*

**N:** In the meantime, the elder son was out in the fields. On his way back to the house he heard the music and dancing. So he called the servants and asked them what was going on. 'Your brother,' they said, 'has come back home, and your father has killed the prize calf, because he got him back safe and sound.'

But the elder brother was so angry that he would not even go into the house; so his father went out and begged him to come in. But he spoke back to his father: 'Look all these years I have worked for you like a slave, and you haven't even given me a goat so that I can feast with my friends. But now this younger son of yours who wasted all your property on loose living has returned and you killed the prize calf for him.'

'My son,' the father answered, 'you are always with me, and all that I have is yours, but now we have to celebrate and be happy because your brother was dead, but now he is alive; he was lost, but now he has been "found".'

## Petitions

**Speaker 1:** Father, we pray for those who are unforgiving, condemning and spiteful.
**All:** Lord, have mercy.
**Speaker 1/2:** Father, we pray for those who are quick to see weakness in others, but slow to see and admit their own faults.
**All:** Christ have mercy.
**Speaker 1/2/3:** Father, we pray for ourselves, because a part of us is like the elder son. We bring that elder son part of us – the resentful, unforgiving, ungrateful part – to you, asking for your healing and forgiveness.

# Rite of Reconciliation

**Priest:** We are not only guilty before God, our Father, and the Lord Jesus for taking the gifts of the Spirit for granted, but we are also guilty before one another. Through our sins, love has grown cold within the body of Christ, within our homes, our communities, ourselves. Therefore, we need to be reconciled not only with God but with each other.

Together we say: I confess .... Our Father ....

*Individual Confession/Absolution*

As the Taize music plays in the background, the priests take their confessional stations. Then the penitents, who wish to confess, go the priest of their choice for individual confession and absolution.

*Concluding rite*

God, the Father of us all, You have forgiven our sins. Help us to forgive one another, and to work together to bring peace to our world. We ask this in the name of Jesus, the Lord.

*Final Blessing*

May our Lord guide our hearts in the way of his Love.
    May Almighty God bless us ....
    The Lord has forgiven your sins. Go in peace.

# Hawaii Reconciliation Rite

This service is based on a Reconciliation Rite I was given by an old man in Hawaii. He had been transported to the Leper Colony there while still a youth and remembered the format which was handed down by the oldest lepers who had been given the rite by Father Damien, the Leper Priest.

Fr Damien asked the lepers to take the day off by themselves with a question sheet which I include at the end of the exercise. The lepers spent the day reflecting on their lives during the past year. In the evening they returned to the chapel with their completed sheets.

**Step 1:**
The service starts with the Taize Tape *(based on the chant 'Stay Here')*.
**Step 2:**
Introduction: Greeting. May God our Father and the Lord Jesus Christ give you grace and peace.

**Step 3:**

Opening prayer: Lord God you so loved the world that you sent your only Son for our health and salvation. Help us now, as we hear again the word of your son Jesus Christ, to acknowledge our failure to follow him and to ask humbly for your forgiveness. We ask this through Christ Our Lord.

**Step 4:**

John 8 – 'The Woman taken in Adultery'. *[Read aloud.]*

**Step 5:**

Holding up one of the reflection sheets the celebrant explains how the lepers were placed in groups of five around grass mats with their reflection sheets. Those partaking in this exercise similarly gather in groups of five around mats placed on the floor with their sheets. The lepers knew they had sinned and one knelt in the centre of the group of five, while the others stood around them placing their stumped hands on the head or shoulders of the one kneeling in the centre, praying for them and asking that the one in the centre might feel forgiven.

**Step 6:**

We do the same. When the one in the centre feels ready they get up and go to the centre of the prayer room where incense and lighted charcoal has been placed. Slowly they place a little incense on the charcoal asking that their prayer rise up to Heaven as an act of homage while they also ask that their sins float away like the incense smoke. They then tear up their reflection sheet and put it into a bowl provided for the purpose.

**Step 7:**

Each member of the group take their place in turn

in the centre of their small group praying for forgiveness while their companions pray that they may receive a felt sense of their forgiveness. When each returns to their group having torn their reflection sheet, they join those standing around the one asking for forgiveness.

**Step 8:**

When all are finished, the Taize music is turned down and all pray the 'I confess'.

**Step 9:**

All say the 'Our Father'.

**Step 10:**

Final prayer: Almighty and Merciful God we thank you for your faithful love and faithful forgiveness. We ask you to help us to show in our lives the compassion and forgiveness that you show us. We make this prayer through Christ Our Lord. Amen.

**Step 11:**

One member of the group is then assigned to take the bowl of reflection sheets outside and burn them while the group continues to pray in silence with the Taize music for as long as they feel is suitable.

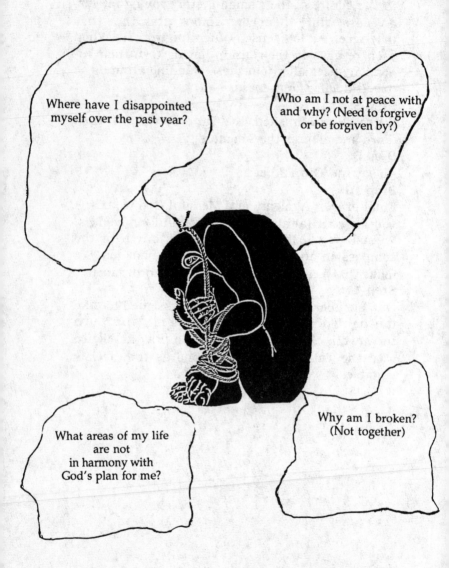

# 3

# Dramatic Change

Tony de Mello, during his retreats, used to say that all good therapy is built around awareness. He would ask us to remember moments when, like Archimedes, we were struck by a 'Eureka!' experience, when some element of our lives, which hitherto has been complicated or tangled, in an instant became clear. It is at such moments that change may be beginning to happen within us. Indeed Tony mentioned that either we changed right there, at that very moment of awareness, or we were unlikely to change at all. He stressed that this attention to change is, in many ways, at the very heart of any retreat based on the Spiritual Exercises of St Ignatius of Loyola.

To develop this concept in concrete terms, Tony reminded us of the film, *Goodbye, Mr Chips*, where the gentle schoolmaster, at the end of his tether and without any control over his class, heads away for his summer holidays. During those holidays, the master falls in love and experiences for the first time being deeply loved himself. He has had a 'Eureka!' experience – one that will turn upside-down his very life – so that when he returns to his school after the summer holidays the boys realise that a transformation has taken place, without being told that anything special has happened and even before the teacher himself understands what has occurred.

To effect this type of dramatic change, we have to come into the now. Tony told us that many human beings function at 10% of their true potential and that 99% of the time we are not operating in the here and now at all. We are either living in the past, reflecting on all sorts of ancient memories and day-dreams or we are focusing on the future, on vague plans which we may wish to bring into being – giving space to aspirations which we hope in a dreamy way might come into being for us. Thus Tony continually urged us to 'come into the now'. Befriend the present moment, he'd say. Become aware of the experience you are going through right now and feel that moment's atmosphere around you, drinking in the sensations it produces within you. He highlighted the fact that in our modern lifestyle we have a tendency to let our experiences become clogged with ideas and analysis, seldom remaining with what is going on deep within us here and now.

In the fantasy exercises and gospel meditations Tony presented, he attempted to provide opportunities where we could 'just be' with our God, or He could be with us, breaking our thinking patterns.

It might be helpful here to say something about what we mean by *Gospel Meditations* and *Fantasy Exercises*. Perhaps meditation can best be explained by one simple word: 'being'. By learning to live only in the present moment, allowing nothing to distract you, when your mind and your emotions are under your control rather than your master, when your awareness is as perfect as possible, then you may be in the meditation state of being, for meditation is about 'being' and not about 'doing'. The term itself comes from the Latin *meditari*, which simply means 'frequent' implying that it should be done frequently but the very imprecision of the word may be a bonus as it allows us to engage in the practice without too many presuppositions or expectations. The Zen Buddhists decribed the routine as 'just sitting' or 'sitting quietly doing nothing'. If the above seems to indicate that meditation is all about doing nothing, that is only partly true. Think of it rather as the time you give to God, a time when He may well gift or grace you with an ability to see clearly what is going on within you, in your own mind, emotions, body, heart. Many books will outline the benefits likely to be obtained by the practice. With faith, you may become more aware of the Living God active in your life, and with that knowledge you may notice an increase in feelings of peace, optimism and self-worth. Added to that you may attain an attitude of independence, self-discipline and a sense of identity. Some participants on weekends and workshops have reported a change in their attitude towards their pain.

If we turn our attention for a moment towards the *Fantasy Exercises* which Tony de Mello led us through we might note that generally we 'position' ourselves within the fantasy in the present tense, ie, being present as if the event were happening right now. This helps us realise that the experience is not just a fantasy but is rather an important expression of ourselves and our life situation. If we afterwards relate the fantasy to another, we may become aware of important details which we were only vaguely aware of during the actual fantasy itself. Also, the listener may notice important items that we ourselves either ignored or overlooked. In fact the very fantasies themselves may open up a space for us to look at aspects of our lives which we would be unable or unwilling to examine otherwise.

Once, Tony told us, he made a Buddhist retreat. His guru used to spend up to ten hours at a time with the group, concentrating only on their breathing, on the flow of air entering and leaving their nostrils. Participants were asked to note the volume of breath entering and leaving their bodies, its hotness or coolness, the roughness or gentleness of each breath they took, its shallowness or depth. During this exercise many participants commented on the boredom or difficulty they experienced and would even question the exercise's validity. In the same way Tony would ask us to persist, saying that he himself had found from experience that the more time he invested in this exercise, the greater he found its value. During this exercise, he said, 'one sort of comes home to oneself'. It was as if one had taken a jam-jar full of muddy water, filled with tiny unseen fish, all swimming around in the murky liquid; and when the water was allowed settle and become still, it cleared, and the life within it suddenly became apparent. Now this sort of clarity or silence within us can be frightening but it allows what is really important inside us to surface. In this quiet space, we thus become aware of important conscious or subconscious aspects of our lives and we may have a

'Eureka' moment of clarity for ourselves. We give ourselves permission to look back at the last few months in our lives and thus discover what experiences have been truly valuable for us and where real fruit has been present for us.

To drive home how this might be done, Tony told us about a Japanese army general who was thrown into prison. Naturally, he was terrified and worried constantly over what his enemies might do to him. So great was his worry that he could scarcely sleep a wink at night. Without warning, however, the words of his Zen Master came back to him in his terror: 'Tomorrow is not real. The only reality is the present'. When the Japanese general allowed himself to believe this, he immediately regained his ability to sleep. The future had lost its grip over him. He became a person who was able to 'be' totally in the present. Many of us spend long chunks of our time regretting what has befallen us up till now or uselessly worrying over potential catastrophes which may overtake us in the future, things over which we have little or no control.

## Fantasy Exercise

### Self Acceptance

Begin by closing your eyes and become aware of your breathing. Do not change your breathing style. Just become aware of it. Now as your gentle breathing begins to relax you, picture somebody of importance from your childhood who loved you a great deal. Perhaps you might focus on your mother or father, or perhaps a favourite grand-

mother. Place them in their most pleasant surroundings, wearing their special rig-outs, and
when they are in front of you in your mind's eye let
them begin to tell you what it was about you that
they really loved in you – what attracted you to
them – and stay with that scene for a minute or so.
Now picture somebody you know at present who
loves you and again let that person express what it
is about you which really attracts them. This may
be some element of your personality or some trait
you have, or some characteristic of yours which is
really attractive. It may indeed be something physi-
cal but let them speak to you about it. Now picture
Christ before you. Do this in any way that is helpful to you. Let Christ speak gently and accept what
He has to say about your gifts. Then very gently
say goodbye to him – and come back to the present, thanking the Lord for the time you were able
to spend with Him. When you are ready, open your
eyes.

*Note. What you are doing during this fantasy is
giving yourself the love and self-respect which you
both need and want. As you do this, you become
more aware of the Spirit's work within you and
gain inner health by means of the positive rather
than negative messages that this fantasy contains.*

## Fantasy Exercise 2

*Your Favourite Place*

This type of fantasy exercise works splendidly with
Leaving Certificate classes in Irish schools. De-
pending on the maturity of the group, more or less

preparation time may be required. I stress here that this preparation of the group is vital. One first has to explain the type of prayer-exercise one is engaging upon, ask the group's permission and support for the venture, and spend as much time as it takes to settle the group through a 'focusing on the breath' exercise, or a 'body awareness' exercise, or a 'becoming aware of the sounds around you' starter.

Settle yourselves. Try to quieten yourselves and become aware of any sounds you can hear outside the room. Perhaps you can make out the sounds of traffic outside, or of the wind gently blowing, or perhaps there are people walking around outside that you can hear, or you might even – if it is very still – be able to hear the sound of a bird singing. Listen for it. Now draw your attention to the inside of the room and exclude all noises outside. Listen for any sounds you can hear inside the room. Perhaps you can hear other people moving, or a chair creaking, or people's breath as it enters or leaves their body. Still yourself now. Just become aware of any sounds you can hear inside the room. Now I want you to draw your attention inside yourself. Become aware of any sound inside yourself. You may manage to hear the gentle sound of the breath through your nostrils, or even sense your heart beat, but just bring your attention within yourself and quietly become still.

Now I want you to imagine that you are walking across some field that you know and that you can picture in your mind's eye. It's a lovely warm day, and you are on your own, but you feel good about it. As you walk down the field you know that a river runs along the end of it, and you can hear the birds singing, and you are happy and relaxed as you stroll along. Now you are coming down to the water's edge itself, and you begin slowly to walk along the bank. Listen to the sound the water makes as it peacefully meanders along, possibly passing over small rocks or moving through reeds. Just enjoy the experience. As you stroll quietly along, you become vaguely aware that some distance ahead of you there is somebody standing in the middle of the river. At some point you recognise that this person is Jesus.

When you get down to the part of the river where Jesus is standing you notice that He is beckoning to you, asking you to come and join Him. Taking off your shoes and socks and noticing that the water is not very deep, you begin to go towards him. The water comes up to your ankles, and then up to your knees, and still He beckons. When you finally reach him, He holds both of your hands and looking into your eyes says, 'never be afraid to reach out to Me.' Then with great gentleness He leads you over to the far bank and together you sit on the grassy slope. As you both watch the water flowing along, you begin to talk to Jesus about your life and how it has been for you over the past months. You muse over the aspects of your life that have been worrying you, or over anything that has been making you anxious or sad, or disappointed or angry, and, as you relate these feelings or events, you begin to feel the pain or worry of these happenings flowing away from you down the river. Take your time here and just be with Jesus, recalling the events, and sensing the worry flowing away.

Now, as you begin to feel the freedom that comes with that release, try to focus on the things you wish for yourself – the inner peace, love, happiness, flowing into you – down that river – and after a time you hear Jesus again beginning to talk to you. He tells you something special about yourself – that is just for you – so you give this moment your best attention and listen for what He has to say.

Now Jesus leads you back across the river and takes His leave of you. You watch Him as He departs, and putting on your shoes and socks, slowly, in your own time, you make your way back along the bank and up through your familiar field, carrying with you the memories you hold and come back to this room here and now.

Again now, I want you to listen for any sounds within yourself and become aware of them. Now extend your attention outside yourself and listen for any sounds you can hear around the room – perhaps the sound of people moving or the scraping of chairs on the floor. Now let your attention go outside the room and listen again for any sounds of traffic or people's voices or birdsong, and then, in your own time, take a gentle stretch and open your eyes, letting them become accustomed again to the light.

*Note. You follow up on this exercise by encouraging those who wish to pair up and share their experience of the fantasy.*

It is also possible to utilise some of the meditation cassette tapes as background material for this fantasy. Experience will teach you when such tapes are a help or a hindrance to the group.

**Tape 1:** *Pachabel Canon – Gordon Jeffries, 1990*
Vital Body Marketing,
The Relaxation Co, Inc.
USA.

**Tape 2:** *The Fairy Ring – Mike Rowland*
94 Longley Road,
Harrow, Middlesex, England.

**Tape 3:** *Awakenings – Tim Weater*
New World Cassettes,
PO Box 15,
Twickenham TW1 4SP, England.

**Tape 4:** *The Lonely Shepherd – George Zamfir*
Phonogram,
50 New Bond Street,
London WI, England.

**Tape 5:** *Silver Wings – Mike Rowland*
Elfinston Cassettes,
The Old Forge Studio, Back Road,
Wenhaston, Halesworth, Suffolk.

**Tape 6:** *Scandalon – Michael Card.*
Sparrow Records,
9255 Deering Avenue. PO Box 2120
Chatsworth, California 91311

THE SPIRIT OF TONY DE MELLO

# Fantasy Exercise with Scripture

*Meeting the Youthful Christ*

Begin this exercise by using one of the preparatory exercises.

Imagine yourself as a young person, aged about twelve. You are very friendly with the youthful Christ who is also about twelve years of age. Set the scene for yourself. It is a peaceful morning, and both yourself and the youthful Jesus are engaged in errands for your mothers. Both of you have been asked to go to the local watering-hole to draw water. As you both make your way to the water, the youthful Jesus puts an arm around you. Feel the closeness between you. He loves something in you that you are not quite aware of. Feel how much He loves you. He understands you better than you do yourself. He knows about your childhood and about how you grew up. He begins to explain events from your childhood and reveals to you their meaning which you may not have understood before.

Now go with the youthful Jesus as He makes His way back to His house. There you find Mary and sit down with her. She lets you know how she loves both Jesus and yourself. You share with her what is in your mind and heart. She wants to hear it. She treats you as she treats her son, being very gentle. When you feel you have gained as much as you can from this exercise, offer up a prayer of thanks to Jesus and Mary for their time with you.

# 4

# Spurters

Fr Tony de Mello continually stressed, during his retreats with us, the importance of self-image and self-belief. He noted that any stray comments of teachers, parents or friends – particularly comments of support or encouragement – can be vital to us in this regard. This building-up of self-image and self-belief in our youth can also greatly influence our image of God in later life. To highlight this point, Tony mentioned an experiment carried out by a noted psychologist, Mr Rosenthal. In a particular educational establishment, as the school year was ending, Rosenthal brought his team into some of the classes and began to tell the teachers about amazing new experiments which seemed to indicate that a new breed of scholar was emerging in today's classrooms. This new type of student he labelled 'the spurter'. The teachers were told that these students were in fact late educational developers and that some of them had been identified in their particular establishment. He gave each teacher a name-list of the 'spurter' students and asked them when school resumed in the autumn to keep a particular eye on the named scholars. He also stressed that on no account should the teachers breathe a word about this experiment to the kids themselves. In reality, Rosenthal was making the whole thing up. Nobody from his team had identified 'special spurter' students but the teachers did not know this. In fact, Rosenthal and his team had chosen at random a number of students' names and this was the list that was delivered to the teachers. One year later the team returned to the school and took IQ tests. They found that every child who had been described to their teacher as a 'spurter' had improved dramatically. When the teachers were asked how they had found the 'spurter' students during the year they used words such as 'keen', 'active', 'anxious to learn'. The teachers had positive expectations for these 'special' children, had asked them more questions than the others, somehow – because they themselves believed the 'spurters' to be exceptional – they had passed on this same belief to the children themselves. The combination of outside positive expectations plus their own new inner self-confidence had produced the change, the dramatic improvement.

So it can be with ourselves and God. If we truly believe that He loves us and that we are somehow fully lovable, the results for us may be equally startling. Tony de Mello consistently hammered home the point to us that most Jesuits – and, by implication, the rest of the world's population – achieve about 10% of their potential. This shocked and disturbed me when I heard it first. Why should it be the case that we under-achieve so regularly? Perhaps feelings of self-guilt have something to do with it.

For years now I have been involved with final-year second level students, conducting their end-of-school retreats. During these retreats one cannot fail to be struck by the feelings of guilt that in-hibit some of the students. In reality, they are ter-rific kids, bright-spirited, alive and hard-working. They do not believe this of themselves. When they are asked for their image of God, they do not indi-cate that they believe in a God of Love, a God who does not demand a return. Their image of God re-minds me sometimes of the one outlined by Fr Gerry Hughes, SJ in *God of Surprises* – the 'Good old Uncle George' God.

Hughes tells the story of two young children who are brought by their parents to visit their rich old uncle George. This gentleman lives in a great castle high on a hill and the children are brought in to visit him in his sitting-room one Sunday afternoon. There he sits, old and stern, wearing a long, white, flowing beard. As soon as they enter he invites the two children to accompany him to the basement of the castle. There he leads them along a dismal corridor with steel-shuttered doors along both sides. These he opens with a great flourish to reveal dramatic flames gushing out and poor mis-erable creatures burning away in flaming agony in-side. To complete the picture, Uncle George takes up a long fork and pokes the suffering creatures back into the flames if they should attempt to escape. Leading the two children back upstairs to their parents, he says: 'Now don't you love me? And if you do not come to visit me every Sunday to honour me, what you saw happening below is ex-actly what will happen to you.'

With that the visit to Uncle George finishes and the parents lead the two terrified children home. Along the way, the parents remind the children that they should always love Uncle George and they promise that they will. Inwardly, they secretly loathe him. So it may be with us. Our fear and self-loathing may spill over into a fear or loathing of God which is very difficult to counter-balance in later life. Self-guilt has taken over. Love – both for ourselves and for God – takes a backseat. So Tony de Mello stressed that we must face the truth, both about our own self-image and about our concept of God. Many are too frightened to tell God exactly how they feel about Him, but the only way to gain liberation is to face the truth. Tell God how you sometimes feel about Him. He knows it anyway. By telling Him in prayer we may well find the experience liberating. The truth may set us free. Tony told us that when he was in charge of young Jesuit students he sometimes discovered that their God-image was similar to the one described above.

To counteract it, he described an exercise which many found helpful. He suggested that the frightened individual conjure up a fantasy picture in their mind's eye during prayer of an 'empty chair'. He asked the student to imagine Jesus sitting in this chair, and the student was to talk with Jesus, telling Him exactly what was on his mind, and in his heart. When all this had been completed, the student was to imagine in fantasy that he moved across to the empty chair himself and he should then respond – as Christ would Himself – to all that he had said. Hearing Jesus respond, through one's one lips, can be a voyage of self-discovery, and is, Tony explained, time very well spent.

Again, Tony suggested a second exercise where

we might converse with Jesus. We should begin this by talking or writing (to clarify our thoughts) all our feelings, starting with the negative issues within us, the resentments, fears, anger that we have found welling up within us. Then, in quietness, we listen to Christ's replies, paying particular attention to His presence beside us, sensing Him holding our hands, hearing Him as He calls out our name and tuning ourselves in to His words of encouragement to us. This may be difficult for some, particularly if we have years of negative hang-ups about ourselves, but by persevering with the exercise we may find Christ gracing us with a felt knowledge of His unconditional love for us.

You may well have experience of what this kind of self-less love and generosity can do to an individual yourselves. I well recall myself how I worked during my early years as a Jesuit with a Sister in a community centre office who had the power of being able to induce tremendous self-respect among her clients. Day after day very difficult customers would attend and they nearly always asked if they could speak with the particular Sister in question. The rest of us in the office were quite happy that they made this request. We knew only too well how difficult it was to satisfy particular individuals but we were amazed when the Sister returned time after time with a smile on her face saying, 'There's something really nice about that person'. For the life of us, the other helpers – including myself – couldn't see exactly what the 'something nice' was. Still, we couldn't fail to notice that each person leaving a session with her walked away with a new lightness of step. Somehow she had seen the Christ in each soul she encountered and had drawn out the goodness within them. Her love assured them that they were good. Something in her eyes communicated the same message and the end result was that they left her presence determined to live up to her expectations of them. God's grace had entered their beings by the simple realisation that at least one other person thought they were 'the best'. Love, then, might be described as seeing that people are good and letting them know that you are on their side.

## Fantasy Meditation

### *The Road to Emmaus*

*Note. As usual, we prepare for this meditation by finding a suitable spot for prayer, quietening ourselves by means of one of the preparatory exercises explained in Chapter One, and placing ourselves in God's presence, asking Our Lady to guide us and grant us the favours we seek. In our mind, we create the following fantasy picture and place ourselves within it.*

'On that very same day, two of the disciples were on their way to a village called Emmaus (and we place ourselves alongside them as they walk and talk about all that had happened in Jerusalem during the past few days). As they talk, Jesus himself comes and walks beside them, but something prevents them from recognising Him. So He asks them, "What matters are you discussing as you walk along?" They stop short, their faces downcast, and then one of them, named Cleopas, begins to explain that they had been talking about Jesus of Nazareth, a friend of theirs, whom the Jewish High Priests had taken and had crucified. "Our own hope had been that He was the one that would set us free, but now, those last remnants of hope have evaporated. And not only that, but some women friends of ours have recently been to Christ's tomb and they found there pieces of his clothing, but of Him they could find no sign". As they related this story, they came to the spot on the road where they had to turn off for their homes, and the stranger made as if to go on farther, but they, sensing something about their companion, pressed Him to stay with them and share their supper. As soon as they sat down to the meal, the stranger began to break bread with them, but immediately He passed from their midst and only then did they know it had been the Lord'.

Reflect now upon the scene. The two walkers had given a lot to Jesus: their time, their friendship, their energy, their hopes, their dreams of future prosperity. They were two ordinary people like you or I. They too had hopes and expectations but, just like us, these hopes – at least in their own eyes – had been dashed. Which of us hasn't been disappointed at some times in our lives, with a friendship shattered, a loyalty thrown aside, a job given to someone else, a business going down the drain, failing where we thought we had succeeded, generally feeling let down by God?

During those times we can readily identify with the walkers along the Emmaus road. We can join them as they say, 'we had hoped' and we can marvel with them as the reality begins to dawn on them that the stranger on the road is also the stranger who has traversed the hard road with us during the rockiest moments of our existence. That self-same stranger who has stridden many a craggy path Himself. The One who understands suffering and aloneness Himself, who has been to all the most difficult places in His own right and who holds us in the palm of His hand during our travails.

## Fantasy Exercise 2

### The Storm at Sea

*(First read Mark 4: 35–41). This meditation/ fantasy exercise is often helped by using a piece of music very quietly in the background ... especially if you are praying the fantasy exercise with a group.)*

Picture for yourself a warm evening and you, and some of your friends, are together at the end of a long hard day. These friends of yours are some of the apostles and Christ is also with you. As you stroll along, perhaps at the edge of a small village, one of the group suggests that it would be a lovely idea to go out rowing in the nearby lake. Christ also seems enthusiastic about this idea and so your little group make their way down to the lake shore. Now keep imagining that as you come to the waters' edge, you can see quite close by one of the fishing boats and you begin to walk over towards it. You take your seat right in the centre of the boat, with Peter, and the other apostles follow you and make themselves comfortable in the various seats. Jesus himself clambers into the boat and as he is exhausted from a hard day's preaching, he settles himself on some cushions right at the back and almost straight away he is asleep.

Yourself and Peter are in the middle of the boat, rowing gently out from the shore. You can see the beautiful evening, with a gentle breeze present and the sun just beginning to go down, and the water lapping quietly around your boat. In the calm and the peace you begin to trail your hand over the side of the boat and allow yourself to feel the cool water running over your fingers. There's a lovely feeling of relaxation about but suddenly you notice that the breeze has begun to stiffen and the water, which up until now had been lapping quietly around the boat is beginning to pound a good deal more fiercely. As you gaze around you, you can see black puffs of cloud beginning to approach the boat and now the wind is beginning to really become quite severe and you look at Peter and his face – the face of an experienced fisherman – is starting to look quite worried. He senses there is a storm approaching and when you look back at the waves you see that they are now beginning to lap in right over the sides of the boat. By this time the wind is really beginning to pick up and great gusts are rocking the boat about. So much water has now come over the sides that you and the others are in danger of drowning. Peter looks at you, fear in his face, and asks you to clamber back to where Christ is sleeping and let him know how perilous things are. So, you begin to crawl back towards Jesus. You grab him by the shoulder, begin to shake him, and when he sleepily opens his eyes you call out to him, 'Lord, save me or I drown'. So, Jesus sits up from his position, stretches out his hand and tells the waves to be calm. Immediately, their rage and fury begins to subside and Jesus looks you straight in the eye and says, 'why did you not trust? did you not believe that I was with you ? ... and I pause, thinking back over the past few months, reflecting on the times when I felt perils in my life ... when I was worried ... when I felt abandoned and alone and unable to cope ... and I just be with Christ ... and listen to his words over and over ... 'why did you fear' ... 'did you not know that I was with you'?

*(You might pause for a few minutes at this point and finally finish the meditation by asking Our Lady to give you a sense of her son's presence in your life and a belief in that presence when next trouble befalls you.)*

## Fantasy Exercise

*Note. This exercise will be most effective if you make yourself comfortable, close your eyes, prepare yourself with one of the basic breathing exercises, and either get someone to read the instructions to you slowly, or read over the fantasy a few times and make yourself familiar with its format so that you do not have to refer to the notes during the exercise.*

Now imagine yourself going for a walk in the cool of evening, with your day's work behind you. You are walking through a wood, and the place is very safe. You are walking along a path, close to a wooded hillside, and you see a small trail up through the trees that leads to the habitat of a well known wise man who is renowned both for his kindness and his wisdom.

As you walk up the side trail, you can just make out a small fire up ahead of you. As you get closer, you can dimly make out the figure of the wise man sitting at the fire. As you approach, you bend down and collect a few small twigs and sticks for his fire. Then you reach the fire. Placing your twigs on the fire, you sit down opposite the wise man and with the help of the firelight, you can make out the features of the wise man. Take time to look at him. Study his features. His face is close to the fire. Study his face. It is kind ... can you make out his eyes ... his expression.

Now ask the wise man a question that has been an important one in your life over the past year. As you ask your question, watch closely for the old man's expression. How does he receive your question? Does he answer it straight away for you and if so, does he do so by word, facial expression or gesture? What kind of answer does he give you?

Now I ask you to do something difficult. Try to become the wise old man. What sort of person are you as the wise old man ... how do you feel and what is your life like? As the wise man, see a stranger coming up the path towards you. This person is, in fact, you yourself as you came up the path a few minutes ago. See the stranger sitting down opposite you. The stranger asks you a question that is obviously important. Take your time before you give the wisest answer you can to the question. How do you feel towards the stranger asking the question? So, slowly, see yourself as you give your answer to this stranger. What do you say? Do you give your answer in words, a gesture or in some other manner?

Now become yourself again. Have you heard the wise man's answer? Have you understood it? What is your feeling now towards the wise man? Soon it is time to go. As you stand up about to leave, the wise man reaches his hand out behind him and searches in a special bag where he has a very particular present for you. He takes it out of the bag and gives it to you for your return journey home. Receive the gift and study it. Has it any particular significance for you? As you turn to leave, you thank the old man and tell him how you feel, before saying your goodbyes and departing for home.

Now slowly become aware of your breathing once again and become aware of the room you have been doing the exercise in. At your own pace, open your eyes and let them become accustomed to the light. Have a stretch and conclude the exercise.

*If you are in a group during this exercise, you might like to turn to your partner and share – insofar as you feel free and able – what happened for you during the fantasy.*

# 5

# The Rescuer

At this point, we've spoken a good deal about the kind of God we are trying to communicate with, the nature of the God we are trying to reach. Let's try to put this into a theoretical framework, one that is practical, that applies to ourselves, to others, to work, to community. To construct this theoretical framework, let us first attempt to sketch the kind of God we are not talking about here. Eric Berne, in his book, *Games People Play*, delineates the varieties of poses we may take up in our relationships with others. He asks us to consider the concept of 'rescuer'. It's the image of God as a 'rescuer' that we first have to discard from our minds. We have to knock on the head any idea that God is there to give us help that we do not want or need.

To explain this concept, Tony de Mello told us the story of Archbishop Roberts, an English Jesuit, who in 1936 was appointed Archbishop of Bombay. Archbishop Roberts found his own appointment to that See slightly amazing for he had very little knowledge of India or the Indian mind, and furthermore when he arrived to take over his new post he found awaiting him a diocese containing a highly developed Church, along with an already formed and gifted clergy. His appointment, he noted, was building up resentment among the local population. In short, the Indians were being given outside help they had neither asked for nor required. To alleviate this dilemma, the Archbishop came up with a clever ruse. He wrote to Rome, telling them that he needed an Auxiliary Bishop, and that a suitable local man called Gracias had now been unearthed. Despite some hesitation on Rome's part, Bishop Gracias was installed as Auxiliary to the diocese and some little time later Archbishop Roberts told his new Auxiliary that he would shortly be going away for a while to undertake important work abroad. In his absence, the new Bishop would be left in charge of the diocese. So it happened that Archbishop Roberts sailed away, leaving the diocese in Bishop Gracias' hands. This situation continued for quite some time, during which the new Bishop dealt more than adequately with his task. After some time it became clear that Archbishop Roberts wasn't coming back. He had seen that the people were being given help that they hadn't asked for and his continued presence would only stifle initiative on their part.

The second type of rescuer that God isn't is a rescuer who gives help where it is not required. Many of us offer assistance which, by its very nature, only stultifies the one being offered help.

Perhaps we men are more guilty of this habit of giving help where it's not wanted than women. I've noticed on numerous occasions that when people come to me with a problem, what they require more than anything else is a listening ear. They are not in fact looking for assistance in the way that I imagined at all. What they require is the healing power of a listener. Someone who will agree with what they are saying, will make re-assuring noises and empathise with them in their plight. What they do not require is someone who will jump in with solutions or answers to problems they themselves feel they do not have. Tony de Mello told us that if he were asked by his Provincial to head for Mission territories he would first ask the Provincial, 'Who is calling me?' Perhaps he would go as far as to write to the local Bishop and check it out. 'Is it true that you want me? What for? And why do you need this help?' He would want to be a helper who intended making himself dispensable and one who would serve temporarily until the present need had been overcome.

Those of you who have studied the Enneagram may discern classic signs of the compulsive helper in this second type of rescuer: the sort of person who is a giver, endlessly looking after others and mothering them, even when they would prefer – and be more helped by – being left alone. We must check ourselves here to see if – under the guise of helping others – we are really meeting our own needs for attention and thanks. If this is the case, we are failing to acknowledge that we need to be appreciated, loved, needed by those around us and somehow we play games in order to hook in from others the love and appreciation we need.

The third type of rescuer comprises people who get involved when, in reality, they would rather not give help at all. Perhaps this type of rescuer can most easily be explained by an example. A priest or religious wearing such visible identity marks as a Roman collar or habit often hears the cry from passers-by, 'Can I have a word with you for a minute, Father?' I have often had the temptation to reply, 'If its about anything other than money, I'll be delighted to talk with you.' Sometimes I actually say that – but often I cheat. I begin the conversation with them and wait with dread for the 'touch' moment to come. In these cases I can feel within myself a movement I do not like – the movement or sense of being a rescuer which travels on to that of feeling a victim. I have allowed myself to become manipulated and know that, in my case at least, those asking for assistance are likely to encounter in me an irritable or reluctant giver. This type of rescuer must learn to say 'no' at times. This is not easy. I fear rejection, being unliked, perhaps even being put down.

The fourth type of rescuer is one who assists others who are not doing all they can to alleviate their own problems. At times this type of rescuer may appear in marginalised areas. The helper moves into the area, begins to see the problems or at least thinks that to be the case, and provides solutions without consulting with, or drawing in, the troubled communities. Those being assisted are not being made or helped to work for what they want.

The fifth type of rescuer is the one who wants something from the rescuee but does not make this plain. This last type of rescuer is perhaps the commonest. You can see it at times in parents when they deal with their children, and sometimes we even attribute this notion to God. In parents it may take the form of harbouring hidden expectations or aspirations but not expressing them. In relationships, the format may be slightly different. How often have we ourselves hoped that our friends would remember our birthdays, or that they had just taken the initiative to phone us first before we had to phone them, but when this doesn't happen we feel bitter, feel like victims. Why did we not tell them what we wanted, and then leave them free to respond in whatever way they wished?

So is God anything like the rescuers mentioned above? I think not. God does not force his help on those who neither require nor wish it, and yet His gifts are open to all. As can be seen in many of the Gospel stories, and can most beautifully be noted in the Pool at Siloh incident, Christ offers his assistance readily, but only having first discovered what the sufferer needs, and whether they truly desire help. Thus, in the Gospel narratives, Christ will often ask two fundamental questions: 'What is it that you seek?' and 'Do you really want to be healed?' When clarity is achieved on those two issues, God's goodness abounds.

## Prayer Exercise

The Sick Man Being Assisted by His Friends (Luke 5:17-26).
*Use the usual preparation and place yourself or the group in God's presence. Quieten yourself by means of one of the quietening exercises. Ask for what you require during this prayer exercise.*

One day, as Jesus was teaching, pharisees and teachers of the law from all parts of Galilee and Jerusalem gathered around Him to witness the power of the Lord. Some men approached this scene, bringing with them a bed-ridden friend of theirs who was paralysed, but finding no way through the crowd, they went up on to the roof of the building and let the sick man down through the ceiling right into the very space where Jesus was teaching.

When Jesus saw their faith, He said to the sick man, 'your sins are forgiven you', but the onlookers began to grumble and said amongst themselves, 'Who can forgive sins but God alone?' Jesus noted this and said to them, 'Why do you question in your hearts?' Turning to the sick man he continued, 'That they may know that I have the power to forgive sin, I say to you, rise, and take up your bed and walk'. Immediately, the man rose and took up his bed and went away glorifying God.

Now quieten yourself and imagine the scene outlined above. Picture Christ in the packed room, His audience held in rapt attention. You are among the crowd and suddenly you begin to notice a commotion and you realise that some strangers are at the edge of the throng and are beginning to haul their paralysed friend on to the roof of the building. Note how they are confronted by difficulties. How they find it impossible to get to Jesus by the normal route. How often have I found the same difficulty? These seekers of assistance are, however, made of sterner stuff than most of humankind. They begin to haul their friend up to the roof and go to a lot of trouble to ensure that he at least comes face to face with Jesus. Imagine the feelings of the patient himself, the embarrassment, the reluctance to cause a stir, the confusion, the doubt about whether all the fuss is worthwhile or not, and then the sick man is lowered down before the concerned face of Christ Himself. Listen to the two questions, 'What is it that you seek?' and 'Do you really want to be healed?' Think of his confusion. He may well not have expected to be faced with the issue so starkly or so suddenly and certainly not before such a large assembly. Put yourself in his position. Become the paralysed person yourself. Take the two questions and assume that they are addressed to you. What is your response? Do I really want to be healed? Here? Now? Stay with those questions for a while before thanking Christ for His interest, time, and concern on your behalf.

## Fantasy Exercise

### A Favourite Place

Either individually or as a group, quieten yourself and in imagination travel to one of your favourite spots, whether it be to the seaside, to a mountain stream, or wherever. You picture this place from memories of your past and make sure it's a place where you can feel happy and at peace on your own.

You might begin by using one of the quietening exercises described in Chapter One and then start the journey, possibly using one of relaxation tapes already mentioned. Let the sounds, smells, colours, features of the location take you over and enjoy being there. Be grateful for this place, grateful for life just now. What comes to mind? The gifts given to you during the past year? The people who have been close to you? The moments when God seemed truly present to you? Occasions or events that now, in retrospect, bore unexpected fruit. By looking backwards, the beauty and value of people and events may well come more sharply into focus and guide you towards where you may wish to spend more time and effort in the future. After some time, say goodbye to the scene and slowly retrace your steps to the place where you presently are.

# 6

# Loving Yourself

In Central China there's a small picturesque town called Yangshuo which is more or less on the tourist trail. There a most unusual event regularly takes place. Each evening, as travellers and tourists begin to make their way down to the edge of the river which runs through the town, a knot of local fishermen paddle their tiny craft, made of thick bamboo canes, to where the tourists congregate. Then they encourage the visitors to part with their hard-earned money and accompany them on the experience of a lifetime.

As soon as you pay your fee, you are assisted into the minuscule fishing craft and are rowed towards the centre of the river. The trips are always undertaken just as dusk is settling on the area and as you make your way out to the fishing-ground you notice a gleaming lantern placed at the head of each boat. Along the side of the vessels, a number of caged birds are perched.

When the fisherman has managed to settle his craft in mid-stream, he begins to release the birds one by one. Each bird is tied by a piece of thread which is attached at one end to the bird's leg and by the other end to the fishing-boat itself. Each bird also has a metal band encircled around its throat, allowing the bird to breathe but not to swallow anything it may catch. As you watch in amazement, fish begin to approach the boat, possibly drawn by the shining light on board, and the birds in turn dive down into the water to grab hold of these fish, returning to the boat with the fish still lodged in their beaks for they are unable to swallow their catch. With a little encouragement from the fisherman, each bird releases its fish and so begins another dive to collect more produce for its master. The birds continue to perform this exercise night after night, despite the fact that they never receive any tangible reward for their efforts.

Tony de Mello, whilst working with us, indicated that similar types of self-defeating behaviour may damage us as human beings. Our tendency to think badly of ourselves, or to run our performances down, make us less effective agents for change and for good in a needy world. We stunt ourselves as ambassadors of Christ. Each one of us has a charism for others, even though we may not appreciate this fact ourselves. So the question now facing us is, 'How can we recognise this charism?' How can we broaden and deepen it?'

Tony de Mello suggested an exercise to help us affirm our own lovableness and in a number of subsequent prayer evenings we have reformulated it as follows: You are invited to climb a mountain in fantasy, and be joined by Jesus there. It's true that in this exercise we are making up a fantasy but we are getting in touch with a deep part of ourselves, and this has a great value. On the mountainside, talk to Jesus, listen to Him. Talk about events which have happened to you during the past month and let Jesus speak to you about what meaning those events might have in your life. If self doubts or negative feelings enter into your fantasy, allow Christ to tell you that He knows your defects, your mistakes, your sins ... and yet He still loves you just as you are. Then reply. As soon as you begin to feel like a prince or princess yourself, you begin to see the goodness in others.

Many of our problems in prayer are not caused by spiritual difficulties. Rather they arise out of human and emotional complications. We are naive to think that prayer will solve everything. Life itself means that we were created by God, to live, to die, to be taken to heaven, but life itself has a habit of throwing up peak and troublesome moments and sometimes it is at life-shattering flash-points that our truest questions surface – that we are most ripe for spirituality. Tony de Mello intimated that on some modern Indian retreats, this factor is taken into account and the participants spend the first four days in 'group-help' for emotional problems leaving the second half of the retreat for silent communication with God. Tony himself engaged in this practice at times as he had found that retreat participants had not really been challenged enough in the emotional and psychologically difficult areas before moving on to more straight-forward prayer. Often, he suggested, retreatants found the first four days most frightening. But to get the most out of these days and make them as realistic as possible he suggested a form of 'journalling' which can be extremely beneficial. The retreatants keep a journal of the happenings in their lives, setting down both the events which have occurred during the past week and what they think these events might be trying to say to them. At first the retreat-ant just logs these events, without being too con-cerned to analyse them. Then they ask themselves, 'Where is my life trying to go? What is my life trying to say to me? Where am I now in my life?'

If this task is being undertaken during a yearly retreat, participants might deepen the exercise by engaging also in a dialogue with a person of im-portance in their lives. To do this, they formulate in their minds a list of people who they know have been important to them. These persons may be either living or dead. They then choose one of these people and begin to dialogue on paper with them, finding out where the relationship is with them at this particular time. They conduct this dialogue from their own particular point of view, jotting down what occurs to them and possibly taking one specific event which they consider to be especially meaningful. After writing down their version of the event, they step into the shoes of the other and re-late on paper how they feel the other person might relate what happened on that occasion. By looking at the happening from both sides, much illumin-ation and meaning may be derived from the exer-cise.

A second elaboration which may prove bene-ficial during this 'journalling' exercise entails dial-oguing with my body. Here I write down how I and my body have been treating each other during the past year. Perhaps my body has been trying to tell me something about how I am conducting my af-fairs. This may manifest itself through repeated ill-nesses, or I may notice on reflection that I get colds, or feel unwell when specific regular events in my life begin to appear on the horizon.

A third helpful addition to the exercise involves logging my dreams. Here I note and make comments on my dreams insofar as I can remember them. To jog my memory, I may keep a note-pad and pencil beside my bed and, immediately upon waking, take notes on the dreams of the night lest the dream be lost. At times during the retreats in India this section of the exercise was conducted in a group. One member of the group was invited to relate a dream whilst the others listened intently and tried to soak up its full meaning. After a brief time for reflection, group members were asked the following question, 'If that were my dream, what would it be saying to me?' Each one in turn answered that question, and some of the reflections often provided illumination to the one who had related the dream in the first place.

A fourth method of broadening the 'journalling' exercise consists of jotting down within the text of the diary significant stepping-stone moments from the past year, ie, occasions when unique spurts of movement occurred. Here I might note paths I did not choose to take and why I chose to ignore or reject them. Has this anything to teach me about myself? How might I more wisely focus my life for the future? In the yearly review, I connect this segment with a 'cross-roads' category where I record choices I made at moments of special decision during the past year, or moments where decisions were made for me. Perhaps now I am ready to take a part I missed some time ago?

The final method for deepening this exercise centres around spiritual stepping-stones. Here I record and reflect upon episodes during the past year when I came to a deeper sense of meaning within myself. Do these episodes illuminate areas of growth for me in the future?

'Journalling' exercise such as this needs to be entered into with a constructive frame of mind, for insights may be given to us which, while extremely useful, may be unpalatable at first taste. Tony de Mello himself told of an exercise he conducted with Jesuit students during their annual retreat where he asked them to retire to their rooms and jot down the names of three people they would miss terribly if they died. He recommended that they follow this by logging the names of three people who would miss them terribly if that same event came to pass. After a time, he said, the group came together again to share its findings. There were many blank pages! This, said Tony, was a salutary lesson for both the students and himself. All realised there was something wrong, and Tony had the embarrassment of having to share with the group the fact that up to eight or nine years before that he himself had very few – if any – close friends, for he found it very hard to believe that he was loved. He had swings, jealousy twinges and feelings of being rejected. Fortunately he also had companions who were very patient with him. They gave him an abundance of unconditional love which he knew as an experience of grace. Its effects on him were incalculable. He changed, became softer. But the biggest change of all was that he began to see attractive people everywhere. Some may get a taste of this through prayer.

So it may be for us. 'Give beauty, beauty,

beauty, back to God, beauty's self and beauty's giver' (Hopkins).

Follow this with two meditations on seeing the goodness in yourself and others.

## Gospel Meditation

### *The Gem in the Field*

Settle yourself down with the usual preparatory exercises and then slowly begin to imagine yourself becoming, if you will, a priceless gem that is hidden in a field. You can feel yourself pressed in on all sides by soil. Perhaps the soil is warm and comforting, or maybe cold and damp, for you will, of course, have your own unique way of experiencing yourself as a gem embedded in the earth and it may remind you of the way you have been formed, reformed, or conformed by experiences within your family, your community, your friends, or your work colleagues.

Stay with that experience of yourself as a gem for a moment, musing over the times of pain and struggle – of being walked over – and think of events from your past when others seemed to step over you, not recognising you. Feel the vibrations of their foot-falls as they tramp about above you.

Then, in the distance, you become aware of movement above you. Christ is out walking in His world, as He loves to do, and everywhere He gazes He notices beauty. You remain hidden, deep in the ground, but you can sense an overwhelming desire arising in you – a desire to be noticed and loved by Christ. Now you become aware of vibrations above your head and you realise that Christ has come over to the very spot where you yourself are hidden in the soil. You dare not even breathe, praying that His attention will turn your way, and then, as perhaps often happens in love, you sense Him moving away, and you can hardly bear the disappointment. He quickly moves away, goes to the nearest town, sells everything He has in His carpenter's shop and purchases the very plot of land that you are buried in, because, in Jesus, there is a tremendous desire also. He has sensed that there is something of real beauty in this place – sensed something of your beauty, your power, your spirit. Thus He returns to the very spot wherein you are hidden and, with very gentle motions, He begins to scoop away the earth, getting ever more close to you. He works with care, not wishing to frighten or damage you, until He prises you with solicitude from your hiding-place, taking you in His hands and looking down at you. His heart goes out to you. He knows your past, knows each side of you, knows everything about you. His only wish now is to share Himself with you. He tells you how He loves you ... what it is He sees in you ... why He sacrificed everything so that you could be His.

Just listen to Him as He begins to share His appreciation, reminding you of your many childhood qualities because some of these qualities are still a part of you. If you experience any kind of resistance towards accepting His words, that is all right, because He appreciates that you may be embarrassed or may have self-doubts.

You might like to take some time now thanking Jesus for the time and trouble He has gone to on your behalf before you finish the exercise.

# A Massage with Christ

*Note 1. I first experienced a form of this exercise whilst on a workshop with Fr Dick McHugh, SJ, a priest who worked with Fr Tony de Mello, SJ, in India for many years. Many groups have found it very beneficial though I should stress that the facilitator needs to feel easy with the group before this exercise is attempted. Also the group members themselves should be asked for their permission before trying this, as some participants may find the very notion of touch disturbing.*

*Note 2. A quiet piece of music such as Ocean Music from Japan should be used as background.*

**Step 1:**
Ask the participants to choose a partner that they feel comfortable with. Name each set of partners 'A' and 'B'. Let the 'A's stand behind their 'B' partners, resting their hands on their shoulders.

**Step 2:**
Let the 'B's close their eyes and begin to realise that Christ is standing close to them ...

**Step 3:**
You, as facilitator, now begin to speak quietly in the first person saying: 'You now begin to appreciate that you have been through a hard workshop/week/course and you are more in tune with the pains, worries, and tensions that past experiences have laid on you. It may well be that the stress of these memories still lingers in your body and, as Christ looks down on you He begins to say that He would like you now to experience something of His life and His Spirit and He is going to

let you feel something of the same now through the gentle hands of your partner so that you will value anew something of your power, your beauty, your strength.'

**Step 4:**

Very quietly, very gently, 'A's begin to massage their partners on the shoulders ... just working their thumbs easily around the neck and up the shoulder blades. As their partners begins to stroke away the tension 'B's sense that Christ is bringing them his peace and soothing away the pain and worries which may have lain heavily on their shoulders. With love, Christ wipes away the tears and the exhaustion of the recent past and if any resentments have built up during these past months, particularly indignation involving people you believe may have done a wrong, these offences are also soothed away. Christ's peace descends upon the 'B's through the healing touch of their partners and they thank God for His affirmation and benevolence.

**Step 5:**

After about ten minutes or so of this exercise, when you gauge the ones receiving the massage have gained what they can from the experiment, you ask them to exchange places with their partners and repeat the exercise.

# 7

# Praying with Scripture

'Self-acceptance,' said Jung, 'including our defects, is the beginning of growth', and Tony de Mello used to quote this sentence during many of his workshops. When we know and accept ourselves we are ready for change. But some do not like to hear this message, and it's not a message that readily springs to mind when we reflect back on the missions and retreats we may have attended in our youth. Our mouths would fall open when Tony told us, 'People do not like to be told that they are OK and even you yourselves do not like it deep-down'. That statement certainly put the cat among the pigeons. If it's true it's a shocker, because the benefits which can come to us if we take this message on board in our spiritual, psychological and emotional lives can be multitudinous.

I recall during my schooldays having a fellow classmate, David, who regularly came bottom of the class during exams. Nothing seemed to go right for him. He was not good at sports, looked weedy, and his only claim to fame was regularly being caught smoking in the lavatories. Then, in fifth year, debating was introduced to the curriculum and volunteers were asked to offer themselves for the first debate. David offered himself, and the result was startling. His first effort was mediocre but he did receive some praise.

Week after week this lad was the first to volunteer for any debate that was scheduled and as the weeks went by his efforts became more and more polished. At first, the sort of comments he heard after the debates were that he 'wasn't bad', and then 'that he had done quite well'. Then this progressed to, 'You really have quite a talent for debating'. David had found something that he could shine at, that he was praised for, and his confidence grew by leaps and bounds. Half way through fifth year he was already a changed student. His overall confidence had grown to such an extent with the praise he was receiving that his school grades had improved beyond all recognition. He had gained enough self-belief to attract a lively girlfriend, and his overall posture exuded a new-found self-esteem. His subsequent career followed a continuing upward curve. Finding something that he was good at, and being acclaimed for it, radically altered his life.

John Holt, in his book, *Why Children Fail* quotes numerous examples in a similar vein and much of A.S. Neill's work in Summerhill, a radical school for troubled children, bears out the same testimony. People do well when they are praised. Is it not reasonable to expect that Christ himself bestows on us the encouragement and acclamation that will ensure our growth?

Throughout the Gospels, Jesus reveals a face of encouragement to us in scenes such as the woman taken in adultery or people born deaf or lame. He wants us to know that he is supportive of our growth at every turn.

During prayer, questions about growth may also be uppermost in my mind. Am I growing? Is my heart opening up in wonder? Am I more alive, flexible, flowing, creative, more open, less defensive? Am I – like Christ – obsessed with doing the will of the Father? Scripture can be a great help to us here.

Before looking at how Scripture might help us, and how we might profitably spend time with it, Tony de Mello cautioned his listeners about its use. Scripture, he said, has been used to do great harm as well as good through the centuries and we only have to look to Iran and other parts of the world today to confirm this fact. It has led to serious errors and no little cruelty in our own times. When picking up the Bible, we might be well advised to imagine that it has the words 'Handle with care' stamped on its cover.

How can we avoid Scripture's pitfalls? Tony told a story of an occupied village during war. The Commander of the occupation troops came to the village's Mayor saying, 'You are shielding a deserter. Give him up in seven days or else!'

The village was indeed shielding a man who seemed good and innocent, and was loved by all. The Council met with the Mayor and local priest and all prayed about how best to resolve their dilemma. Finally it was decided that their best option was to hand the fugitive over. 'It is better that one man die and the nation be saved.'

Years later a prophet passed by that place and asked, 'What have you done? Twenty years ago God sent a saviour to your country and you gave him up to be tortured and killed.'

'What could we do?' pleaded the Mayor. 'The

priest and I looked at the Scriptures and acted accordingly.'

'That was your mistake,' said the prophet. 'You looked at the Scriptures when you should have looked into his eyes.'

Whilst reading the Scriptures therefore, keep your compassionate heart and your commonsense. Saint-Exupery, in his book, *The Little Prince*, says something similar when the fox reveals his secret to the Little Prince. 'We see best with the eye of the heart!' You need a heart to listen to the Scripture.

## Exercise One

Some years ago, I made an eight day retreat alone in the beauty of Connemara. As the retreat reached its sixth day, I noticed that a silence descended upon me and that tiny portions of Scripture could bestow great meaning. I was reflecting on Christ's Passion and, as the sixth day went on, one line of Scripture kept reverberating in my heart – 'Lord, if all the others leave, I will never desert you'. On the seventh day of the retreat I found myself again chewing over just one sentence, 'And they all ran away.' I added to this, 'And so did I.' Just two lines over two days.

Tony recommended this form of prayer with Scripture highly. So try it. Allow the Gospels to lead you into silence, and then to understanding. Let the word or phrase resound in your being, fermenting in your very essence. A variation of this exercise is the Benedictine method of prayer, a form of vocal praise which launches us into mystical heights through use of mind, heart and body.

You choose a rich passage such as Saint John's Gospel: 7–37.

The last day of the feast was the most important. On that day Jesus stood up and said in a loud voice, 'Whoever is thirsty should come to me and drink'. Speak these words aloud. Etch them in your heart. Perhaps a word, or a phrase, strikes a chord with you. Recite the word in the form of a mantra ... 'Whoever' letting it sink deeper and deeper, not thinking of the meaning but giving your thirst full play. When satisfied move on and work silently or aloud on the word. 'Whoever'. 'Do you really mean that, Lord?' 'Could it be me you are talking to?' 'I'm angry, Lord, because I feel I've come to you many times already without sensing your presence' or 'Yes Lord, I've come before and I know you've filled me with graces, and for that I want to give thanks'. Phrases like these may come at the beginning, but afterwards your responses may well become deeper and richer so that no words will be needed to express them. Stay in that silence as long as it seems profitable.

This method may also be used in a scriptural reflection on Christ's introduction of the Eucharist (Matthew 26:26). 'Now as they were eating, Jesus took bread, and blessed, and broke it, and gave it to the disciples and said, "Take, eat; this is my body"'. Stay with the words. Let them sink in and impart their full meaning.

Cardinal Basil Hume tells a lovely story about a visit he made to a refugee camp in a war-torn country. As he was being escorted around the camp a small boy came up to him and firmly grasped him by the hand. During the visit, the

Cardinal relates, this small boy refused to let go of his hand and it appears that the lad had only appeared in the camp that very morning having recently lost both his parents in the war. When the time came for the visit to finish, the Cardinal began to climb aboard a departing train but he found it almost impossible to extricate his hand from that of the boy. The lad had found a protector. All day he had held on to a hand that offered security and with his free hand he occasionally rubbed his stomach. Leaving him behind was one of the saddest incidents in his whole life. As the Cardinal related it afterwards, the boy had pinpointed the two essential needs he experienced in his life. The desire for love and the need for food. The very gifts Christ has bestowed on us during the Last Supper.

# Meditation

*The Marriage Feast at Cana*

**Step 1:**
Settle yourself comfortably in your favourite prayer place and use one of the quietening 'awareness of breath' exercises to prepare you for prayer.
**Step 2:**
Read over a Scripture passage slowly. Take John 2:1: 'On the third day there was a marriage at Cana in Galilee, and the mother of Jesus was there; Jesus also was invited to the marriage, with his disciples. When the wine failed, the mother of Jesus said to him, "They have no wine".

'And Jesus said to her, "Woman, what has this to do with me? My hour has not yet come."

'His mother said to the servants, "Do whatever He tells you."

'Now six stone jars were standing there, and Jesus said to the servants, "Fill the jars with water", and they filled them to the brim. He said to them, "Now draw some water out, and take it to the steward of the feast". So they took it. When the steward tasted the water – now wine – he called the bridegroom and said to him, "Every man serves the good wine first; and when men have drunk freely, then the poor wine; but you have kept the good wine until now."'

Stay with the scene for a while. The following questions or ones similar to them may begin to fuel your prayer.

– Lord, when and where have I been in similar positions to the one described above?

– Can I think of any situations during the past year when I felt I needed nourishment, and felt abandoned by you?

– Were you in fact present as you were at Cana?

– Did I lack your mother's perseverance and faith?

– Did I believe that you would, in fact, intervene on my behalf?

– Did I, like your mother, have the courage to make my hopes and aspirations known to you?

– When you asked for action from me as you did from the servants, did I take steps to help myself, even though I could not comprehend the reason for your promptings?

– Finally, when you did intervene, did I notice, respond and thank you for that?

# Fantasy Exercise

## The Rosebush

Find a comfortable position and close your eyes. Turn your attention away from outside events and notice what is going on inside you. Notice any discomfort, and which parts of your body emerge into your awareness. If you become aware of a tense area of your body, see if you can let go of the tensing. Now focus your attention on your breathing and feel the air move in through your nose or mouth. Feel it move down your throat, down into the pit of your stomach and as you release it allow any tensions which may have built up within you to evaporate.

Now become aware of any thoughts or distractions that may have come into your mind. What are they, and what are they like? Now imagine that you put all these thoughts and distractions into a glass jar and examine them. Slowly, in your fantasy, empty the jar, allowing all the thoughts and distractions within it to drain away.

Now, in your fantasy, imagine that you are a rose-bush. Become a rose-bush and discover what it is like to be this shrub. Let the fantasy develop on its own and see what you can fathom about being such a plant. What kind of rose-bush are you? Where are you growing? What are your roots like and what kind of ground are you in? Perhaps you are in a garden or on an isolated hillside. Are you on your own or are there other bushes around you? What do you experience and what happens to you as the seasons change? Continue to discover even more details about your existence as this rose-bush, how you feel about your life, and what happens to you. Let your fantasy continue for a while.

Having completed this fantasy exercise you may discover aspects of yourself that you would have been unable or unwilling to discern if you had faced the questions head on. Perhaps the idea of being isolated in life struck you, or the fact that your thorns repelled others, or that you needed the nourishment of the soil, or the local community you were planted in was highlighted dramatically. Some people have mentioned that times of hardship, such as winter, which seemed unproductive at the time, allowed them to rest and regain their strength before branching out with new foliage in the spring. One person revealed that the snows of winter, which might have killed them, in fact acted as a cleansing agent in removing green-fly and destructive forces from their environment. Many such insights may come to you through this exercise and on its completion you may either reflect on it privately or share your perceptions through group discussion. Tell other group-members about your fantasy in the present tense, as if it were happening now. For instance, 'I am a solitary rose, growing alone on a hillside, giving out my beauty and scent without its being noticed', or 'I am rooted in a populated place, with many other rose-bushes around, and their aroma encourages me to flower to my full potential'.

# 8

# Using Fantasy in Prayer

Those of you who are familiar with the Spiritual Exercises of St Ignatius of Loyola will recall what they often referred to as the 'composition of place'. St Ignatius recommends that we reconstruct in our mind's eye the place where the action we are about to contemplate takes place. In the Spanish text this means not so much a putting together or composition of place, but rather a more direct 'seeing of the place'. Put another way, it is not only the place that you compose but you attempt to compose yourself as you see the place in fantasy. Through the use of fantasy, many feel refreshed and strengthened as they manage to recapture not only the scene they are praying over in their imagination but also the emotions originally experienced in that scene.

Fantasising did not begin in this century of course. Plato wrote about his fantasy cave and Christ Himself invited His friends to fantasise. Recall His use of fantasy when He invited His listeners to picture how a poor woman lost one of the coins from her dowry and turned the house inside out to find it. He then taught them that the almighty Lord acted the same way with a lost soul. Use of fantasy within prayer has a long Church tradition behind it. Many of the saints made use of it. We only have to think of Teresa of Avila who attended Jesus in His agony, Francis of Assisi who took Jesus down from the Cross, or St Anthony, who played with the Child Jesus, to realise that getting in touch with Christ through fantasy assists us – as it did the saints – to get in touch with our deepest selves. We live in two worlds, the world of sense, of our senses, and the world of images, of fantasy. At times we naively think that only our senses put us in touch with the real, forgetting that images and fantasies may also reveal truths to us. They can be a vehicle to enlighten us to realities about ourselves which might otherwise be too painful to contemplate. Just as Jesus and the saints drew understanding from fantasies, so can we.

Without the use of fantasy in prayer we limit ourselves. Modern physics tell us that the world is very different from what our senses alone suggest. Jung has said, 'Get people in touch with their fantasies and you'll cure them'. Tony de Mello told us of the sensational things which can happen to us if we let go of ourselves – being careful, of course, to distinguish imagery from sense-reality. He related how he once worked with a group of young Jesuit students in India. One of the group was a stony-faced chap not greatly liked by his companions. Tony gave the group a fantasy exercise to complete. He asked this particular individual to become a mountain stream. As the student related his adventures afterwards he explained that he had, as requested, become a stream. At first he had thought of himself as rather small. 'In time, however, I became larger, gathering strength, rushing down the mountainside and dropping over waterfalls. As I made my dash towards the sea, I became majestic. Children came and played along my banks. I came to some flowers and swirled with delight around them. I knew these flowers were meant to be a gift to me and I began to treat them so.'

Tony insisted that this student changed in his dealings with others shortly after he completed this exercise. We all carry within ourselves powerful positive images. If we can get in touch with these images we will never be the same again after an experience such as the one described above. If we begin in God's presence and let ourselves stay there, fantasising turns out to be a simple and very easy form of prayer. To help us understand how fantasy prayer works, Tony gave us an exercise for ourselves.

To attempt this, go back in time to the place of your birth. History prepared for this event as it planned for the birth of Christ. Think first about how your parents were chosen, how their personalities complemented each other. Talk to God about why He gave them these personalities to produce you. Christ Himself came with a message for the world. What is your message? Ask the Lord for help in trying to work out what your message should be. Perhaps you will be helped in your summation by a word or an image. Look back on your life's events both big and small and for those say 'thanks'. Look forward in expectation and surrender and say 'yes'. The angels sang and rejoiced at Jesus' birth. Did you hear them singing for yours?

Some people take to fantasy prayer very easily. It has to be admitted that others do not. On retreats and prayer workshops a number insist that they find it very difficult to conjure up any images in fantasy at all. Our imaginations can be fairly threadbare. When we try to bring our whole self to resonate with 'the truth' we find that we can see things as they are, but have difficulty resonating with them in fantasy. So are there any hints which might help us along the fantasy road?

As a starter exercise, you might begin by looking out the window. What did you see? 'A tree'. Now close your eyes and, in your fantasy, wave a wand over the tree. Change it in your imagination. Don't use your mind to paint the picture. Rather let your imagination run riot. After a time you will begin to form a picture of the scene outside.

We can use the skill of fantasy to change emotions which may have built up in us through past events. Take, for example, an event from your past life where you felt you were wronged. Perhaps you feel that you have been under-achieving for some years now in your life or work. Something has gone wrong. Find out what that might be. When exactly did this feeling of lethargy begin to manifest itself?

'Well, only in the past four or five years.'

'Did anything happen?'

'Well, my Superior did place me in a job that I felt unsuited to and unwilling to undertake.'

So go back. Find out where you are still angry. Try to understand where the angry feelings have come from. The ways we view situations that have befallen us affect us mightily. If we can change our perception of a past event we may well be able to alter our interior feelings about it.

Tony de Mello told the following lovely story. A

man went into a restaurant in anticipation of a really good meal. He had been looking forward to the event all day. As soon as he sat down and the menu was presented to him, he selected tomato soup as his starter. He had been thinking about this moment all day. The waiter explained that the kitchen had run out of tomato soup but three or four other soups were available. Alternatively, he could try some of the other starters on the menu if he so wished. Now, as Tony explained it, the man had a choice. He could either rant and rave about the deficiencies of the restaurant and allow this small irritant to spoil his entire evening, or he could say, 'Never mind, my second choice is almost as enjoyable as my first', thus ensuring that the lack of tomato soup had almost no effect on the pleasure he obtained from the evening.

So utilise fantasy and you will find it an excellent introduction to contemplation and to meditation. On school retreats and with adults I commonly use fantasy exercises. At first, I felt a bit foolish doing this but I noticed that almost all groups – and these included adults, Leaving Certificate students, priests and teachers – benefited from the experience. Most people enjoy being freed to roam in imagination.

## Fantasy Exercise 1

*(This is based on The Blessed Trinity Meditation presented in the early part of the Spiritual Exercises of St Ignatius of Loyola)*
**Step 1:**
Prepare yourself. Come into the presence of the

Blessed Trinity. Allow the Three Divine Persons to enfold you in Their love and imagine that they invite you into Their company. Be aware of how you are before the Godhead, musing over your feelings, desires, longings, hopes, thirst for God in your life.

**Step 2:**

In your imagination think back to the time just before Christ's coming to earth when the Three Divine Persons looked down on our earth and saw what a mess it was in. Wars abounded. Sickness and plagues were rife. What chance had goodness got against such evil? Can anything be done?

Think about how the Three Divine Persons were filled with compassion, hearing the cries of the poor, the oppressed, those struggling to live under unjust and oppressive systems. Observe the Father, Son and Holy Spirit as they try to work out the best possible course of action which they can take.

**Step 3:**

Notice the Son of God offering Himself for the daunting task ahead and watch as the Three Divine Persons select Mary to be the Mother of Jesus.

**Step 4:**

Try to observe the Three Divine Persons as they gaze at the world of today struggling for peace, joy and justice. Now see the Trinity looking on you ... noticing you ... loving you ... seeing your potential for good in today's world, inviting you to be part of the mission of Jesus as He brings the good news to those around you.

**Step 5:**

Notice your own response, your feelings, your

thoughts and speak openly to God about these from the bottom of your heart. How do you feel drawn to respond to the invitation of the Trinity as they ask you to co-operate with them in saving the world? Watch as they comment upon all the good you have done in your lifetime, and particularly the good achieved in the past few months. Think of the good which you are still to do for God.

**Step 6:**
Notice the Three Persons beckoning you and drawing you into Their company and then pray for the ability and enthusiasm to respond to their invitation and challenge.

## Fantasy Exercise 2

This is an exercise based on an event from St Margaret Mary's life, when she was told by her director to ask the Sacred Heart what her spiritual director's most recent sin was.

In this fantasy I imagine a person who commits a sin so dreadful that no one can name it. It is the worst sin ever, and the sinner does it over and over again. At length, he determines to stop. He goes to God and says, 'I repent of that sin'.

God asks, 'What sin?' and when the person names it God says, 'I have been waiting for you to name it and stop. I am glad you finally have. Go and sin no more.'

The person is overwhelmed with joy and for a while he desists from the sin, but then, being weak, he falls prey to the same temptation again. Feeling completely demoralised, but determined to try again, he returns to God explaining he has fallen prey to the same sin again. And God asked, 'What sin?' Reflect over this scene prayerfully.

## Fantasy Exercise 3

*The Song of the Bird*

Quieten yourself and become aware of your breathing. As you become aware of the silence within you, I want you to imagine that you are a bird in song, moving around one of your favourite places.

**Segment A:**
- what kind of a bird are you? are you brightly coloured or rather dull? do you like your colouring?
- listen to your song. Is it sweet to your ear?
- where do you live? in a nest, tree, roof-top or elsewhere?
- do you fly a lot and how high do you fly?
- what do you enjoy most about being a bird?

**Segment B:**
- picture yourself with other birds ... are there many around ... are they the same species as you or different?
- do you like to fly with the flock or alone?
- what messages do you give or take from these birds?
- what are the reactions of the other birds to you?
- take time to get a sense of yourself among these birds.

**Segment C:**

– now continue to see yourself as a bird in your favourite place on a beautiful summer's day ... listen to the birdsong around you ... what are you doing on this idyllic day?

Taste your freedom, freshness and joy.

**Segment D:**

– after some time some children come into the scene you have painted for yourself.

– what is your first reaction and are the children saying anything to you or about you? If they are saying something, what is it?

– are they doing anything to you? Are they gentle or cruel?

– do you fly away or charm them with your bird-song?

**Segment E:**

– after some time allow one of the children to catch you and hold you in their hand ... what does the child do to you? do you enjoy it or would you prefer to be away by yourself in flight?

**Segment F:**

– the child ties one of your legs with a string, holding the cord but letting you move. What's your feeling now that you are tied?

– do you try to escape or are you satisfied with your bondage?

**Segment G:**

– Now become a person again and recall what happened for you during the exercise.

– compare your life as a bird with your daily life as a person.

– become aware of similarities and dis-similarities.

– stay with your deepest self and see where you desire to change, to grow or to be more free.

*If this exercise is being done in a group, members may like to share how they got on at its completion.*

# 9

# Discernment ... Finding God in all Things

The spirituality of St Ignatius of Loyola, on which much of Tony de Mello's thinking was based, quite often deals with discernment. This notion of discernment comes from the Greek root, *diakrisis* and means sifting through or putting things in order. It indicates more than just good judgment. It is the process through which one pays attention to the promptings and movements of the Inner Spirits as they interact with the human heart. We observe these 'Movements of the Spirit' in order to judge which of them are coming from God and which are coming from the Evil Spirit. In this way, we may be guided wisely towards our best future paths in life. Discernment is a way of coming to know God's will and keeps us close to the mind and plan of God for us. It is essentially about noticing the call of the Holy Spirit within. In the terminology of John Carroll Futrell, SJ, discernment helps us separate the 'wheat' of movements for loving actions from the 'chaff' of those movements that steer us towards selfish unlove. In scriptural terms we might recall a verse from Deuteronomy (30:19) 'I have set before you life and death, blessings and curses; therefore choose life'. Or again, 'Test the Spirits to see if they are from God' (John 4:1).

But how, concretely, do we find out God's plan for us in everyday life? To assist us here, Tony de Mello used to tell a story from Saint Ignatius' own life. He recalled how Ignatius, whilst still young, and having led a life seeking worldly pleasure and fame, was badly wounded in the leg during a wartime skirmish for his patron. His companions, fearing for his life, carried him to his castle in Loyola in order that he might recuperate. Ignatius himself tells us that during his convalescence, he spent his time in idle fantasy thinking about rescuing noble ladies in distress. One day, tiring of this game, he sent down for some books from the Loyola castle library. The poor maid who received this request could only come up with two volumes, *The Imitation of Christ* and *The Lives of the Saints*. Ignatius says that he spent his mornings idly dreaming about achieving great worldly fame through feats of special daring, and then, in the afternoons, having enough of these fantasies, he turned his thoughts to undertaking wonderful deeds for Christ in a similar fashion to the undertakings he had read about in the *Lives of the Saints*. On reflecting upon this period of his life some months afterwards, he says he was very much struck by the fact that when he thought back about how much pleasure the worldly fantasies had given him some months previously, those fantasies now tasted like 'sawdust in his mouth' whereas when he brought his mind to bear on how the lives of the saints had affected him, those memories now tasted like 'honey on his lips'. It was as though, Saint Ignatius himself says, 'God was dealing with me in the same way as a schoolteacher might deal with a child'.

'He instructed me'. This insight formed the basis for St Ignatius' discernment of Spirits. He learned how he might judge which areas of interest would prove profitable for him in the future. He might, by reflecting back on his experiences, be able to see where – in future – much fruit for him might lie. In other words, in T.S. Eliot's phrase, 'the end is where we start from'.

By spending time reflecting on our own past unique faith journey and on its patterns, we can discern something of God's plan for us. You may be able to think of incidents in your own life where this scenario proved true. I recall an incident in Africa some years ago when a Jesuit priest whom I was working with wanted me to experience something of the local culture. As he was otherwise occupied himself, but knew that a wedding feast was taking place in a distant village that night, he suggested that I take his motorbike and make my own way to the feast in order that I might experience the colour and music of the occasion for myself. 'You will have no difficulty finding the place for the path from here to there is constructed over sandy scrubland without roads but it is marked out by small white sticks implanted every few hundred yards of the way'. Aided by this knowledge I set out. Sure enough, as he indicated, the white sticks could clearly be spotted dotted every so often along the route and this enabled me to reach the village shortly before sunset and in good time for the wedding feast. As my colleague had promised, the event was memorable indeed and well worth the trip. In fact the whole event was so engrossing that time slipped by unnoticed. When I next looked at my watch many hours later much time had slipped by and complete darkness had fallen. Fearing that my absence might cause worry, I began the return journey by motorbike, knowing that I only had to follow the white sticks to safely return to my starting-place. For a time, all went well. Then suddenly, in the inky blackness, the bike – without warning – suddenly stopped. In my enthusiasm to start out on the journey, I had forgotten to check the petrol supply and it had now run out. All alone, in the middle of the African plain, I began to hear all sorts of noises, either real or imagined. I could hear lions and tigers – I have subsequently discovered there are no tigers in Africa – and I also noticed that the front light of the bike was losing light rapidly as the battery wore itself out. The rest of the night was a terror. I had to switch off the light to conserve power, and then, switching it on for a few moments, I picked out the next white stick along the route. Switching the light off to conserve energy, I made my way through a series of short dashes from white stick to white stick. As soon as I reached each stick, I would pause for a few moments, switch on the light for a second, pick out the next white stick, and having again turned off the light, made a dash for it. Sometimes I was lucky and I reached my objective. At other times I realised that I must have missed my point of reference for I had gone too far and I would thus have to turn around and retrace my steps by means of the tyre mark I had created until I returned to my last known reference point. Eventually I managed to get back into my colleague's village as dawn began to break. I remember clearly that the last few hundred yards of the journey brought me over a high vantage point, and looking back, I could clearly make out the route I had travelled. It was easy to see, looking back, the occasions when I had gone off the track.

In discernment, we look backwards in order to focus ourselves on the best way forwards for us. God has a dream for our world, and encourages us into being a community of love. If we can co-operate with God's plan by responding to the inner drawings of the Spirit we will assist our own peace of mind. We know that God speaks to us in many interior as well as exterior ways. In prayer, we pray for guidance – seeking God's wishes. We pray about problems. What comes to mind and stays there may well be the answer. 'What the inner voice says will not disappoint the hopeful soul', says Friedrich von Schiller.

A helpful method of focusing on areas of future growth is the daily examination of conscience which involves finding God in our day. One method of attempting this is by means of a five-fold plan. First, I become aware of the presence of God in my life and whilst breathing in and out I recall God's presence in me. The air I breath is a sign of God's closeness to me.

Secondly, I think back over my day and notice what I'm grateful for. Hour by hour, remembering people or events, moments of peace or joy, I dwell on God's goodness to me.

Thirdly, I try to notice moments in my day when I wanted God's help and light, when decision-making proved difficult or when I required strength in bad times.

Fourthly, I reflect on times of sinfulness or faults in my day. Here I feel sorrow for what has been mean or sinful in my day and I ask for forgiveness.

Finally, I look ahead and pray for the times to come, people I may meet, work I have to do, and I ask for guidance about the wisest course of action for me concerning new roads that may be opening up for me. I attempt to turn my stumbling-blocks into stepping-stones. Perseverance in this exercise is a great element of success. If you only knock long and loud enough at the door, you are sure to wake up somebody and if that door appears to slam shut it may well mean that God is pointing to an open door further along the road. I end with a prayer to the Holy Spirit.

In attempting to discern the finger of God in my life, it is unreasonable to expect that stumbling-blocks to our inner freedom will not be encountered. However painful it may be, these blocks must be faced and worked through. During his workshops, Tony de Mello talked much about such blocks as being partly the consequences of Original Sin and partly a result of our personal history. Unless we remove these blocks, he indicated, they will prevent us from looking back in order to focus ourselves for the future. He talked first about repressed anger which may be one of the commonest problems. People who 'explode' indicate this. They are all bottled up. If you are angry, and you let the anger flow through you, you remain in control. The most beautiful flowers need a lot of muck. So with anger, feel it always and release it in a healthy way. When you are expressing it, do so with care.

It can be great to have outlets. You probably have your own, but a good walk along a sea shore, letting out the occasional yell (when nobody's around, of course) can be very therapeutic. When working as a member of a team, it may be essential to report such feelings in order to build up trust. It may be that you do not report the anger at the time, but a little time later, telling about it when you are in control of the situation. When we are not able to report it, the anger may build up so use a phrase such as 'A certain behaviour of yours makes me angry'. A simple revelation like this can resolve the problem. 'Don't let the sun go down on your anger' (Eph. 4, 26). Tony mentioned something similar about fear. If we allow it to crystallise within us, it may prevent us from making any positive strides in our lives.

Whilst working near Pearl Harbour last year I came across a veteran of the Japanese Pearl Harbour attack during the Second World War. He related the following incident which illustrates how fear can paralyse our lives. He told me that his left arm was paralysed and he was sent to Carl Rogers to see if anything could be done about the complaint. Rogers got this ex-navy gunner to talk about his war experiences and he related how he had been aboard his ship on that fateful Sunday morning when the Japanese planes began to attack. As the man took up his battle station he realised that the machine-guns on board were turned in the wrong direction to confront the approaching enemy. As he relived the scene, graphically illustrating how he tried to turn the guns around, he suddenly noticed that his arm – which had been paralysed for very many years – was beginning to move. His fear had frozen him for all those years. By getting in touch with the cause of his fear he was suddenly helped to free himself.

## Gospel Meditation

*Simeon (Luke 2: 2 –32 )*

Start by reading the text.

'There was a man whose name was Simeon, and this man was righteous and devout, looking for the consolation of Israel, and the Holy Spirit was upon him. And it had been revealed to him by the Holy Spirit that He should not see death before he had seen the Lord Christ. So inspired by the Spirit he came into the temple; and when the parents brought in the child Jesus, to do for him according to the custom of the law, he took him up in his arms and blessed God and said, "Lord, now let thy servant depart in peace, according to thy word; for mine eyes have seen thy salvation which thou hast prepared in the presence of all peoples, a light for revelation to the Gentiles, and for glory to thy people Israel."'

**Step One:**
With the usual preparatory exercises, begin by placing yourself with Simeon at the door of the temple. Imagine the scene. An old man, full of faith, sitting there for many years trusting that God will not let him die before the promise made to him has been fulfilled. Thus, inspired by the Spirit, he goes each day to the temple. So you sit with him today on the hot, dusty, temple steps. The old man

is righteous, old, patient, looking for consolation. As he waits for the Lord he knows that the Holy Spirit is with him.

But the Lord didn't come quickly ... did not come at a time he expected. Simeon must almost have given up hope of ever meeting the Christ-child but now, as you sit beside him, you notice the quality of his peering and searching beginning to change.

**Step Two:**

On this day Simeon had come to the right place, at the right time, with a listening heart and an eagle eye and now suddenly his heart jumps within him. Be with him now and listen to him as he mutters to himself. He has waited years and years for this very moment. Imagine his feelings as he spots the couple coming towards the temple – a child in their arms. What are your feelings? Be with him as he dashes across and takes the Christ-child into his arms. 'Now that I've held you in my arms, I can go in peace'. You take the Child in your own arms now also. What is your feeling as He comes to you? Talk to Mary and Joseph about the hopes you have now that He has finally arrived. He's a light to the world, but a light in your life also. What areas of your life do you ask Him to uncover for you? When you have stayed with the scene for as long as is profitable, give Him back to His parents and gently end the meditation.

# 10

# Re-awakening

In all of Fr Tony de Mello's workshops, retreats, videos and books we sense the importance of personal inner freedom. This is what I call the spirit of re-awakening and it is, for me, the very essence of what Tony was trying to bestow. One might say it was his gift to people of today. To illustrate this spirit, Tony was fond of quoting the works of Gandhi and extolling the spiritual element therein. He recalled Gandhi saying, 'I hold that the aim of human life is the vision of God. To attain this a man must be ready to sacrifice everything'. Gandhi was concerned about the vision of God. His words are strangely similar to those given by St Ignatius of Loyola to St Francis Xavier from Saint Matthew's Gospel: 'What does it profit a man if he gains the whole world and loses his own soul?'

This question may seem very single-minded. But many of the founders of religious orders had this 'one-pointedness' of vision themselves. To obtain this 'one-pointedness' a certain quality of inner freedom must first be achieved and many of us are not as free as we think. We have been programmed.

Where does this conditioning come from? It is deep-seated and often comes from the 'scripts' we have had imprinted within us from our earliest experiences. Tony de Mello quoted examples from his own family life to illustrate this. He recalled how one day he drove a religious sister to her train after one of his retreats. The Sister had a special ticket which would be useless if she did not catch a particular train. As they drove towards the station everything seemed to conspire to delay them. It appeared less and less likely that the Sister would catch the train she sought. When this realisation dawned on Tony he panicked. But the Sister stayed calm and did in fact catch her train as it also was running late. Tony recounted afterwards how the Sister had acquired her relaxed attitude from her early family training. Within her family, missing a train was considered a minor irritant. Conversely, in Tony's own family, such an occurrence was considered to be a disaster.

If your family gets angry with problems, or depressed, or pretends that problems are not there, that's the 'life-message' you learn. Tony himself told us that when he paid a visit back home to his parents, years after he began life as a Jesuit, he found to his surprise and somewhat to his horror that he was the 'spitting image' of his parents. His attitude to strangers, to guests – who were sometimes considered to be something of a nuisance – to sex, to other religions, to different races, to money – whether one should spend it or save it – how to use time, his attitude to work, were all conditioned. His reactions were embedded in him, in his guts, and it took years to work out what beliefs were really his and which had been bludgeoned into him.

These 'life-scripts' make us unfree and may require considerable work by us before we are to be liberated. I remember an incident which occurred shortly after my ordination. I was living in a small, inner-city community with a wonderful older colleague who was very well known and liked by the poor of the city. One morning, when this man had already gone out to work, one of his tougher-looking clients came hammering at our door. I was repairing a door-lock at the time as it had recently been smashed and I was dressed in a very old pull-over. Taking me to be a repair-man, the visitor demanded to know when my colleague would return. On being told that this might not be for some time he barged in and sat down on a stool in the hall-way with a mug of tea, watching me at my work. After a while he began to look around our flat which on that cold and wintry morning, suffering from the effects of a recent break-in, did seem rather drab.

'I'm told the Jesuits live here,' he said. 'They must be mad, and the particular fellow I'm looking for may not only be mad but is also a mean sort of man. He's from Wicklow, of course, and most Wicklowmen are mean'.

I agreed that the Jesuits did indeed live in the flat and that they were quite possibly mad so he followed this up by asking, 'Do you know any of the priests yourself?'

When I told him that I did know some of them quite well his eyes began to narrow.

'You wouldn't be a Jesuit yourself by any chance?' he asked, and seeing my face turn red he followed this up by changing his whole demeanour and sticking out his hand saying, 'Wonderful men who live here and very generous too. Would you have a few bob to spare?'

The change he managed to effect within himself in such a short time and for the sake of a few shillings was wondrous to behold, even if it was only skin deep. Should we not be prepared to put in an equal effort to reform our childhood 'scripts'?

If someone came to Tony with a neurosis, he asked himself where their 'script' had been formed. In motoring terminology, he wondered who was driving the car? Is it you who are driving or your family history? It takes a great deal of courage to stop the car, to ask the passengers to get out, whether it be the pope, or your teachers, or parents, or any significant others in your life. It takes courage because you will now be alone, and perhaps feel fearful of driving single-handedly.

A good rule of thumb to detect whether a 'truth' or 'life-script' is really your own is this: when somebody contradicts you, do you get all hot and bothered and emotional? If so, Tony said, it is a sign of indoctrination, of truths that have been taken from – or imposed by – others. If the beliefs are really your own, you will be much readier to change, to adapt. The free person is the one who listens and learns from others and is ready to change and adapt where necessary. So question everything. Prevent indoctrination by asking yourself two priceless questions: 'Why?' and 'Why not?'

Tony told us of the famous Bishop Butler who spoke of the great changes he had seen in the Church in the last fifty years. He said there were things I dreamed of in the 1930s, but dared not ask why? So many were thrown out of the Church for asking why? And they asked only out of love for the Church and out of loyalty to Jesus. So Tony suggested adopting this principle – 'If I don't see it, I don't accept it.'

When asking these two great questions we must do so without aggression. Saint Paul did this, in love, when he attempted to correct Saint Peter in the early days of the Church over the matter of circumcision. Without Paul, men would all be circumcised today. Disloyalty is an attitude. Questioning is not. The live fish swims against the current. The dead one floats with the tide.

We cannot always rewrite harmful 'life-scripts' on our own. We sometimes require fellow travellers to re-awaken us. This was never more evident to me than when an old leper told me his life-story on Molokai, Father Damien's leper colony in the Hawaiian Islands. The man had been diagnosed one fateful day when he was only six years of age. The medical inspector arrived at his school and after examinations a note arrived at his home stating that the boy would be removed from his parents and transported to the colony at noon the next day. The poor child found himself being dragged screaming and kicking away from kith and kin without any prior warning and placed among complete strangers in the leper settlement. For a month, he said, he hovered between death and life. He had lost his will to live. Then one morning two kind leper-women took him to a nearby steep cliff face which separates the leper section of the island from the section inhabited by the healthy. As he looked up at the cliff-face, his mother suddenly appeared. He could remember, some sixty years later, his mother's image as if it were yesterday. She was dressed head to foot in a long black cape, her face surrounded by a hood, and she carried a bible in her hands. From this, in the sweetest voice he had ever heard, she began to sing him psalms. For about an hour this performance continued and then, with a wave of her hand and tears in her eyes, his mother stepped back from the edge of the cliff-face and disappeared. The leper told me how the two kind leper-women who had taken him to the spot brought him back the way he had come and gently whispered to him, 'Now you have to make a choice. Only you can decide whether you want to live or die. Your mother has done all she can for you.' At that moment and influenced by their kindness and concern for him, he decided to put all his energies into living. When the old man told me the story he said that in the sixty years since the event had happened, he had never regretted his choice. By their action, the two leper-women had re-awakened the desire for life within him.

Re-awakening this desire for life within us is a delicate business. A certain subtleness is required to ensure that the desired result is obtained without destroying the self-respect of the recipient. An old man in the west of Ireland tells the following story about himself that illustrates that his father was a past-master at the art. He has never forgotten the incident. He vividly recalls how each day in his youth he had to return homewards after school in the company of his schoolfriends. Their path took them through lovely countryside. His mother was an exacting sort of woman and expected the boy home shortly after school finished. She then had a hot meal ready for both himself and his father. The old man recounted, however, that particularly during the summer evenings the trip home was laced with interesting events. Sometimes his fellow pupils would stop to chase cows, to fish, or just sit and idle their time away in the sun. This infuriated the mother. The dinner she had specially prepared for both himself and his father regularly got burnt. It also meant that his father, who had broken off work specially to be with the family, had to hang around while the dinner was destroyed. One day, the old man remembered, the family had convened a meeting. His father explained how upset his mother became when the meals were ruined. From now on the boy would have to make it back on time or suffer the consequences. Some days later, the lad stopped once more on his way home and on finally reaching his destination he suddenly remembered the promises he had made. He walked in with fear and trepidation. From the table the most beautiful smells assailed him. His mother had prepared a favourite meal of steak and onions. But a shock awaited him. Only two portions were on the table, one in front of his mother and one for his father. He, being late, had only a glass of water in front of his place. In silence, and ever so slowly, his mother began to set about her dinner. Each bite seemed a delight. The boy knew he deserved his fate. He was going to go without and be hungry for the night. At that moment, in total silence, his father placed his own meal in front of the boy and indicated that he should eat. Slowly the boy realised that his father was going to do without his own portion. 'It was,' said the old man, 'the most difficult meal I had ever eaten. Each bite seemed to take an age to go down. I knew my father was sacrificing himself for me. He may not have liked my thoughtlessness towards my mother but he still loved me. He hated the sin but he loved the sinner and hoped that I might change. It was a lesson I never forgot.'

With God, that same loving forgiveness applies. He has the power to bring good out of evil. Accept God's loving forgiveness and let it re-awaken the 'best you'. There is a legend about Saint Peter after he denied Christ. He felt so badly about himself and what he had done that he believed Jesus could never forgive him. With this thought in mind, he went to Jerusalem and poured out his heart to Our Lady. 'What must Jesus think of me? I can never expect him to forgive me now.'

Mary answered, 'Remember Peter, what He Himself said to you. Not seven times, but seventy times seven. Jesus has forgiven you long ago. Now you have to learn how to forgive yourself.'

Do not allow guilt to disempower you. Tony de Mello stressed that guilt is selfish, self-centred. It is pride turned on its head. It is regretting, not so much the damage caused, as the fact that I am at fault. Remember that a sin is forgiven before it is committed. So forgive yourself, believe in yourself, knowing that Christ has forgiven you already. The most crippling unbelief is unbelief in yourself. If it is not tackled, it can stultify your desire for re-awakening. If you love life, life will love you back.

This gift of loving life must be nurtured. Last Easter, I was invited up to a liturgical centre in Northern Ireland for their Easter celebration of midnight Mass. Lent had been long and cold and many of the faces I encountered there seemed in need of encouragement. The Mass itself had been arranged so that it coincided with the first light of Easter Morning. Thus, in total darkness the celebrant led us outdoors to a local mountain-top. A great pile of sticks had been gathered there and the preacher began the ceremony by comparing the season of Lent to life itself. Both are dark and gloomy at times, he stressed, but then quoted an ancient Irish proverb, 'If you can keep a green branch alive in your heart at the hour of darkness, then the Lord will send a bird to come and sing from that branch with the dawning of the day'. As he spoke that sentence, the Easter fire of sticks was lit and as the flames shot into the sky, three elements simultaneously fused to create a marvellous image. The first streaks of dawn light touched the sky and were accompanied by both the fire and a burst of birdsong which would have moved a heart of stone. The hope that had been kept alive during the dark days of Lent was awakening to the song of the bird, heaven-sent to sing to us from the green branch kept alive in our hearts. It was a picture Tony de Mello would have understood completely. An image of re-awakening he himself tried to foster.

# Gospel Meditation

*Mary Magdalene Washes the Feet of Jesus*

Mary Magdalene Washes the Feet of Jesus (John 12:1–8).

Using one of the preparatory exercise, first read the Gospel passage outlined and then place yourself with Mary Magdalene as she ministers to Our Lord. Watch as she stands beside Jesus, weeping at her past sins and wishing to offer some sign to Him of her love. Note how she takes the costly ointment and anoints his feet, wiping them dry with her hair. She does not let the fact that there are on-lookers put her off. She is rewarded by hearing Jesus saying, 'Truly, her sins are forgiven because despite her many sins, she has loved much'.

Mary could only have engaged in this act because Jesus' words of forgiveness had first touched her. His love had gone deep down inside her. She had heard Him say with words of warmth, healing and consolation, 'Come to me, all you you who are burdened and heavy laden and I will give you rest'.

So enter into the scene. Be with Mary Magdalene as she kneels beside Jesus, seeking rest for her weary heart. See how she finds comfort in His presence. Mary was able to wash the feet of Jesus with her tears mainly because she had experienced a similar washing of her own feet by Jesus; not literally, but she somehow knew that Jesus had spent His whole life cleansing all of us with His tears. She knew He had entered all of our pain, loved us so deeply that our pain became His pain, our burdens became His burdens.

So let Jesus kneel with you now, washing away your pain, your burdens, your bad moments from the past. Feel His tears upon your feet, listen to His sobs, note the look of caring and tenderness He has for you. His is a heart large enough to embrace the whole world and will embrace you also. Let scenes of pain from your past life come to the surface. This is a safe time to be with Christ in past scenes of hurt, pain, loss or trouble that you have needed to grieve over but were unable or unwilling to do until now. Allow the warmth of Jesus to fill you up and let your pain flow out. Finish now by hearing Jesus' words, 'What would you have Me do for you?' Ask for healing and release with the words, 'Lord, that I might be healed'.

# BIBLIOGRAPHY

**Barry, SJ, William A.**, *Paying attention to God: Discernment in Prayer,* Notre Dame, Ave Maria Press, Indiana, 1990.

– *Finding God in All things: A Companion to the Spiritual Exercises,* Notre Dame, Indiana: Ave Maria Press, Indiana, 1991.

**Barry, SJ, William A. and Connolly, SJ, William J.,** *The Practice of Spiritual Direction,* The Seabury Press, New York, 1982.

**Cooke, Grace,** *Meditation,* The White Eagle Publishing Trust, England, 1955.

**Davis, Roy Eugene,** *An Easy Guide to Meditation,* Mercier Press, Cork, Ireland, 1988.

**De Mello, SJ, Anthony,** *Sadhana – a Way to God,* Gujarat Sahitya Prakash, Anand, India, 1978.

– *Wellsprings – A Book of Spiriture Exercises,* Gujarat Sahitya Prakash, Anand, India, 1984.

– *The Song of the Bird,* Gujarat Sahitya Prakash, Anand, India, 1982.

– *The Prayer of the Frog,* 2 volumes, Gujarat Sahitya Prakash. Anand, India, 1988.

– *One Minute Wisdom,* Gujarat Sahitya Prakash, Anand, India, 1985.

– *The Heart of the Enlightened,* Collins, Fount Paperbacks, London, 1989.

– *Taking Flight,* Doubleday, New York, 1988.

– *Contact with God – Retreat Conferences,* Gujarat Sahitya Prakash, Anand, India, 1990.

– *Call to Love,* Gujarat Sahitya Prakash, Anand, India, 1991.

**Fontana, David,** *The Elements of Meditation,* Element Books, Dorset, 1991.

**Green, SJ, Thomas H.,** *Weeds Among the Wheat: Discernment – where Prayer and Action meet,* Notre Dame, Ave Maria Press, Indiana,1984.

**Hebblethwaite, Margaret,** *Finding God in All Things: Praying with St Ignatius,* Collins, Fount Paperbacks, London, 1987.

**Hughes, SJ, Gerard,** *God of Surprises,* Longman and Todd, London, 1986.

**Lonsdale, SJ, David,** *Eyes to see, Ears to Hear: An Introduction to Ignatian Spirituality,* Darton, Longman and Todd, London, 1990.

**Maryland Province of the Society of Jesus,** *Place Me With Your Son: The Spiritual Exercises in Everyday Life,* Maryland Province of the Society of Jesus, Maryland, 1985.

**Puhl, SJ, Louis J.,** *The Spiritual Exercises of St Ignatius based on Studies in the Language of the Autograph,* Loyola University Press, Chicago, 1951.

**Valles, SJ, Carlos,** *Unencumbered by Baggage,* Gujarat Sahaitya Prakash, Anand, India, 1987.

**Wilson, Paul,** *The Calm Technique,* Thorsons, London, 1987.

**Zanzig, Thomas,** *Learning to Meditate,* Saint Mary's Press, Christian Brothers Publications, Winona, Minnesota, 1990.

### Audio Cassette Tapes

*Sadhana,* (12 Tapes)
*Wake Up To Life,* (12 Tapes)
*Wellsprings,* (8 Tapes)
*De Mello Satellite Retreat,* (4 Tapes)
Issued by the We and God Spirituality Centre, Fusz

Memorial, St Louis University, 3601 Lindell Blvd, St Louis, Mo 63108.

**There are three videos by Fr Anthony de Mello, SJ, available:**

*Wake Up, Spirituality for Today*, With Anthony de Mello, SJ, Tabor Publishing, PO Box 7,000 Allen, Texas, 75002, USA.
*A Way to God for ToDay*, Tabor Publishing, PO Box 7,000 Allen, Texas, 75002, USA.
*Rediscovery of Life*, Available from Veritas Ltd, Dublin.

## More Interesting Books

# Body-Mind Meditation
### A Gateway to Spirituality

**Louis Hughes, OP**

You can take this book as your guide for a
fascinating journey that need not take you
beyond your own hall door. For it is an
inward journey, and it will take you no
further than God who, for those who want
him as a friend, lives within. On the way to
God-awareness, you will be invited to
experience deep relaxation of body and mind.

*Body-Mind Meditation* can help you
become a more integrated balanced person. It
is an especially helpful approach to meditation if the pace of life is too fast for you, or
if you find yourself frequently tense or exhausted.

# An Easy Guide to Meditation

### Roy Eugene Davis

Meditation is the natural process to use to release tension, reduce stress, increase awareness, concentrate more effectively and be open to life. In this book you will learn how to meditate correctly for inner growth and spiritual awareness. Specific guidelines are provided to assist the beginner as well as the more advanced meditator. Here are proven techniques used by accomplished meditators for years: *prayer, mantra, sound–light contemplation, ways to expand consciousness and to experience transcendence.*

Benefits of correct meditation practice include: deep relaxation, stress reduction, inner calm, improved powers of intelligence, and strengthening of the immune system. People in all walks of life can find here the keys to living life as it was meant to be lived.

**Over 100,000 copies sold.**

# PETER CALVAY HERMIT

## Rayner Torkington

This is a fast-moving and fascinating story of a young priest in search of holiness and of the hermit who helps him. The principles of Christian Spirituality are pinpointed with a ruthless accuracy that challenges the integrity of the reader, and dares him to abandon himself to the only One who can radically make him new. The author not only shows how prayer is the principal means of doing this, but he details a 'Blue Print' for prayer for the beginner, and outlines and explains the most ancient Christian prayer tradition, while maintaining the same compelling style throughout.

**Over 34,000 copies of this bestseller have been sold.**

# Create Your Own Health Patterns

John L Fitzparick

Disease has to be understood in its literal sense dis-ease – a lack of ease and an expression of conflict. In general we create our own sickness and if we are capable of recreating our own sickness then we are capable of recreating our own health. Once inner peace and harmony are re-established nature has the power to repair itself and good health should ensue.

Fr John Fitzpatrick sees every human being as having the innate ability to heal both self and others. Healing takes place in all cultures, within all belief systems and among all types of people. In some this ability is developed to a greater degree. It is an ability which can be enhanced and developed through practice and through the use of certain disciplines.

# CONTEMPORARY THEOLOGIANS

## JAMES J. BACIK

*Contemporary Theologians* is intended for all those who want to participate more fully in the great conversation about the religious concerns which tug at the mind and heart. James Bacik discusses the work of 20 theologians and the first grouping contains the three giants of Catholic systematic theology – Karl Rahner, Bernard Lonergan and Yves Congar. They are followed by four more systematic theologians who have worked out of the broad Catholic tradition, Hans Urs von Balthasar, Edward Schillebeeckx, John Macquarrie and Hans Kung. Next comes Karl Barth and Paul Tillich, two influential Protestant theologians. Reinhold Niebuhr and John Courtney Murray are then linked together as public theologians. They are followed by four political and liberation theologians, Johann Metz, Gustavo Gutierrez, Rosemary Ruether and Martin Luther King. The next grouping consists of authors who are not professional theologians but excercised great influence on religious thought: Alfred North Whitehead, Jacques Maritain and Teilhard de Chardin. Finally, Martin Buber and Mohandis Gandhi, influential thinkers who represent religious traditions other than Christianity, complete the list.